SpringerBriefs in Computer Science

Series editors
Stan Zdonik, Providence, Rhode Island, USA
Shashi Shekhar, Minneapolis, Minnesota, USA
Jonathan Katz, University of Maryland, Maryland, USA
Xindong Wu, Burlington, Vermont, USA
Lakhmi C. Jain, Faculty of Education, Sci, Tech & Maths, University of Cambera, Adelaide, South Australia, Australia
David Padua, Urbana, Illinois, USA
Xuemin Sherman Shen, University of Waterloo, Waterloo, Ontario, Canada
Borko Furht, Dept Comp & Electrical Engg & Comp Sci, Florida Atlantic Univ, Boca Raton, Florida, USA
V.S. Subrahmanian, Dept of Computer Science, University of Maryland, College Park, Maryland, USA
Martial Hebert, Pittsburgh, Pennsylvania, USA
Katsushi Ikeuchi, Tokyo, Japan
Bruno Siciliano, Università di Napoli Federico II, Napoli, Napoli, Italy
Sushil Jajodia, George Mason University, Fairfax, Virginia, USA
Newton Lee, Tujunga, California, USA

More information about this series at http://www.springer.com/series/10028

Rae Earnshaw

Research and Development in Art, Design and Creativity

 Springer

Rae Earnshaw
Centre for Visual Computing
Faculty of Engineering and Informatics
University of Bradford
Bradford, UK

School of Media, Arts and Design
Wrexham Glyndŵr University
Wrexham, UK

ISSN 2191-5768   ISSN 2191-5776   (electronic)
SpringerBriefs in Computer Science
ISBN 978-3-319-33004-4   ISBN 978-3-319-33005-1   (eBook)
DOI 10.1007/978-3-319-33005-1

Library of Congress Control Number: 2016945372

© The Author(s) 2016
This work is subject to copyright. All rights are reserved by the Publisher, whether the whole or part of the material is concerned, specifically the rights of translation, reprinting, reuse of illustrations, recitation, broadcasting, reproduction on microfilms or in any other physical way, and transmission or information storage and retrieval, electronic adaptation, computer software, or by similar or dissimilar methodology now known or hereafter developed.
The use of general descriptive names, registered names, trademarks, service marks, etc. in this publication does not imply, even in the absence of a specific statement, that such names are exempt from the relevant protective laws and regulations and therefore free for general use.
The publisher, the authors and the editors are safe to assume that the advice and information in this book are believed to be true and accurate at the date of publication. Neither the publisher nor the authors or the editors give a warranty, express or implied, with respect to the material contained herein or for any errors or omissions that may have been made.

Printed on acid-free paper

This Springer imprint is published by Springer Nature
The registered company is Springer International Publishing AG Switzerland

Foreword

Rae Earnshaw is somewhat of a Renaissance man, with interests ranging from art and creativity through computing to academic and research administration. He has served as professor of electronic imaging, as dean of a school of informatics in a university central administration and as professor of creative industries. This book brings together these experiences in the context of two significant and pervasive trends in higher education.

The first trend is that of interdisciplinarity. More and more research and education is at the boundaries of traditional disciplines, rather than within the silos of traditional academic organisational structures of colleges, schools, departments, etc. Rae's particular interest, as reflected in this book's title, is art, design and creativity – but with an implicit subtitle of "computers in support of art, design and creativity". Rae is well prepared to discuss this subject: he has a long record of European Union and other interdisciplinary funded research projects, and his remit in his current visiting professor of creative industries position at Glyndwr University is to facilitate interdisciplinary creativity between artists, designers and technologists.

The second trend, not mentioned in the title but an important theme of the book, is the increasing emphasis by national research funding agencies on accountability and metrics. The trend is typically driven by pressures on research funding budgets that leads politicians to want measures of success. As a UK academician, Rae has lived through a series of increasingly intense periodic (typically every 5 years) research audits used to allocate block grants to UK universities. The first and fifth (final) chapters draw heavily on this valuable experience.

Chapter 2 has an informative discussion that will be useful to academics wanting to understand the research style in art, design and similar disciplines.[1] The chapter

---

[1] What is meant by "art, design and similar disciplines"? Quoting from a citation in Chap. 1 – "The following is an illustrative list of subject areas within practice, theory and history of art and design that the sub-panel expects to assess: animation; applied and decorative arts; architecture; conservation, the study of materials and techniques; crafts; creative and heritage industries; critical, historical, social and cultural studies; entrepreneurship and enterprise; film and broadcast media; fine arts; landscape and garden design; museology and curatorship; photography; policy,

is informed by the author's experience with UK's every-5-year evaluation of all universities – to determine block grant funding levels. In the USA, we (fortunately) don't have a similar process – we have no equivalent to block grants. I especially enjoyed the discussion of practice-led research – as found in the arts and design – as distinct from the traditional methods of science and technology. It is important to understand the two approaches in order to work across art and technology!

Chapter 5 can be thought of as a continuation of Chap. 2, with a focus on the UK research audit process and how it accommodates the practice-led research of art and design.

Each of the five chapters has an extensive list of references and suggestions for further reading; these are valuable pointers for those wanting to take a deep dive into any of the book's topics.

Read this book (or selected chapters thereof) if you are:

- An academic administrator seeking to understand how to judge research in art and design.
- A faculty member wanting to do research across the boundary between art and design on the one hand and science and technology on the other.
- Involved in making national-level policies about how to assess research productivity, especially but not limited to art and design.

Atlanta, GA, USA   James D. Foley
March 2016

---

management and innovation studies; product design; spatial, two- and three-dimensional design; textile, dress and fashion; time-based and digital media; visual and material culture".

Preface

My involvement in computer graphics began in the early 1970s, and I have always been interested in how good ideas are arrived at. Do they come out of the blue? Do they come from careful thinking of how we've got to where we are now? Do they come from conversations with research group members or research peers or from conferences? Do they come from a detailed review of the literature? I can think of a number of instances where a conversation with a visitor to the university – or someone working in another discipline – led to some new ideas in my own research areas. At times, a creative spark of insight can appear to be, to a large extent, serendipitous and dependent on just the right combination of circumstances and the availability of key information. At other times, it comes out as a detailed analysis of a particular piece of research.

Involvement in a number of large interdisciplinary European projects over the years which were involved in research and development in a number of application areas, such as multimedia assets for design, collaborative visualisation over networks and virtual entertainment, led to a number of important results. Three of these are VISINET, VISTA and VPARK, and they are summarised in the book. One key point which arose out of these projects was collaboration and the ways in which technology could support this. Therefore collaboration and communication form one aspect of the book (Chap. 3). The relevance of this to collaborative design is clear, and this is detailed in the book. What is less clear is how this may apply to art and the creation of artistic works. However, many artists now work in collaborations and exhibit in a collaborative way and also utilise technology, and this is summarised in the text.

A second key aspect of the book is creativity (Chap. 4). I have always been interested in how creative ideas and outcomes are arrived at. What kinds of environments produce positive creative results? What stimulates creativity? Can technology play a role in stimulating creativity? What are the factors which generate creativity? What blocks and inhibits creativity?

Thus collaboration and creativity are the two central themes of the book. The other principal aspects are how research and development in art and design may be formulated, and framed (Chap. 2), and then evaluated and measured (Chap. 5).

The situation in the UK with regard to the support and audit of research is used in this book as a case study to illustrate the key issues and principles. It is recognised that the situation in other countries may be different to a greater or lesser extent. However, it is hoped that this case study is useful, irrespective of the reader's immediate context.

A further important aspect is the valuable contribution that art and design makes to the scientific and technological enterprise and vice versa. However, valuing interdisciplinary contributions, and performing research in this area, remains a difficult challenge in most countries and organisations. Hierarchical structures and funding mechanisms are heavily orientated to maintaining the status quo around the existing disciplines. This needs to be changed and transformed if the potential for knowledge advancement is to be fully realised.

The University of Bradford pioneered the area of digital media in the mid-1990s by tripartite collaborations between technology, art and design, and media and broadcasting. It was done by setting up a new academic department because it did not sit easily within existing academic disciplines and structures. It was very successful in attracting students and also meeting the needs and requirements of industry. It also highlighted the benefits and advantages of interdisciplinary collaborations.

I have also had the opportunity as a professor in the School of Media, Arts and Design at Glyndwr University over the recent years to think about these aspects and published a number of papers in collaboration with the faculty.

The book is being published in the Springer Briefs series which are summaries of the state of the art in a particular area. It is being published as a print book and also an e-book. In the latter, each chapter will be downloadable separately. This is why the References and Bibliographies appear at the end of each chapter. Thus a chapter contains the main points in the area and the reasons for their significance. It is not intended to examine each of these points in detail – there is no space to do this. However, the interested reader can follow up in the References or Bibliography if they wish to.

It is hoped that this book makes a useful contribution to an important area of discussion and debate.

Bradford, UK   Rae Earnshaw
March 2016

Acknowledgements

Thanks and appreciation are due to all those who read draft versions of the chapters and provided comments to improve technical content and readability. These included Jack Bresenham, Stuart Cunningham, Mohan de Silva, John Dill, Peter Excell, Richard Guedj, Alan Haigh, Bob Hopgood, Karen Heald, David Johns, Susan Liggett, John McClenaghen, John McDermott, Mick McKigney, Stewart Milne, Bob Parslow, Tracey Piper-Wright, Alec Shepley, and John Vince. However, responsibility for the final text rests with the author.

Thanks are expressed to colleagues and students at the School of Media, Arts and Design at Wrexham Glyndŵr University, Wales, for many useful discussions and reviews of various chapters.

Thanks are expressed to Jim Foley for providing the Foreword to the book.

Thanks and appreciation are also due to Springer for assistance and support with the production of the book and e-book.

March 2016   Rae Earnshaw

Contents

1 Strategies for Research and Development in Art and Design 1
   1.1 Introduction 2
   1.2 Research in Art and Design 2
   1.3 The UK Research Excellence Framework 2014 3
   1.4 Strategy in the European Union and National Science Foundation .. 6
   1.5 Strategy in the UK Research Councils............................... 7
   1.6 Strategy in the UK Arts and Humanities Research Council 9
   1.7 National Endowment for Science, Technology and the Arts (NESTA) 9
   1.8 Current Research Strategies in Universities 10
   1.9 Increasing Selectivity in Research and Research Funding........... 12
   1.10 Large Scale Collaborative Research Versus Individual Research 13
   1.11 Conclusions 15
   Further Reading 15
   References 16

2 Models for Research in Art, Design, and Creativity 19
   2.1 Introduction 19
   2.2 Research in Art and Design 20
   2.3 Practice-Led Research.. 23
   2.4 Models for Research in Art and Design 25
   2.5 Models for Research in Creativity 26
   2.6 The Relationship of Art and Design to Technology.................. 27
   2.7 Conclusions 28
   Further Reading 28
   References 29

3 Collaboration Methodologies in Art and Design 31
   3.1 Collaboration Across Traditional Disciplinary Boundaries........... 32
   3.2 Ancient Civilisations 33

3.3	Design Education	35
3.4	Art and Science Collaboration	35
3.5	Crowd-Accelerated Development	36
3.6	Visualization and Collaboration	37
3.7	Contemporary Collaborations	40
3.8	Conclusions	43
Further Reading		44
References		44

4 Creativity and Creative Processes in Art and Design ... 47

4.1	Defining Creativity	48
4.2	Historical Examples of Creativity	49
4.3	Interaction and Creativity	49
4.4	Digital Environments and Creativity	51
4.5	Enhancing Creativity	54
4.6	New Media in Cyberworlds	55
4.7	Interaction and Collaboration	56
4.8	Crowd Accelerated Innovation	56
4.9	Can Creativity Be Developed?	57
4.10	Can Creativity Be Measured?	57
4.11	Barriers to Creativity	58
4.12	Conditions for Creativity to Flourish	59
4.13	Creativity and Big Data	59
4.14	Creativity and Discovering the Unknown	60
4.15	Percentage of GDP Spent by a Country on Research and Innovation	60
4.16	Research in Creativity	61
4.17	Creativity and Paradigm Shift	61
4.18	Conclusions	63
Further Reading		63
References		64

5 Research Monitoring and Audit in Art and Design ... 67

5.1	Introduction		67
5.2	Assessing Research Quality		70
	5.2.1	Research Quality	70
	5.2.2	Research Outputs	71
	5.2.3	Research Impact	72
	5.2.4	Research Environment	74
	5.2.5	Interdisciplinary Research	74
5.3	Results of the Evaluation		75
5.4	Lessons from the Overview Reports		77
	5.4.1	Strengths	78

		5.4.2	Weaknesses	78
		5.4.3	Observations	79
		5.4.4	Discussion	79
5.5	Staff Selection			79
5.6	Use of Metrics			80
5.7	Use of Metrics in Art and Design			81
5.8	Review of Metrics by the Higher Education Funding Council			82
5.9	Evaluation of the UK Research Excellence Framework 2014			83
5.10	Distinctive Considerations for Creative Disciplines			83
5.11	Monitoring and Audit			84
5.12	Cost-Benefit Analysis			84
5.13	Changing Patterns of Publication			85
5.14	Conclusions			85
Further Reading				86
References				86

Chapter 1
Strategies for Research and Development in Art and Design

Abstract It is a requirement of many higher education institutions and research organisations throughout the world that they develop corporate strategies in order to specify organisational objectives and the timescales for their delivery. These normally include statements about mission, vision and values. Such strategies also have to satisfy national and statutory requirements where national functions, standards, and funding are involved. These corporate strategies will include research strategies for those areas of the institution engaged in research. Thus many organisations and institutions formulate research and development strategies for their Institutes or Schools of Art and Design in order to synchronise with the overarching strategies of the organisations to which they belong. These Institutes or Schools may be supported by research groups within the area of art and design that seek to capitalise on the academic strengths of their constituent members and their individual and collective research achievements and aspirations. This may also involve external partnerships in areas where joint work is taking place, whether with another School in the institution, an external sponsor, an artistic agency, a funding body, or an external research group. Most projects funded by the European Union require the participation of different research groups from different countries, where complementarity of research specialisms is required in order to enable the project to deliver to the wider canvas defined by the proposal. Such collaborations enable larger research projects to be undertaken and a more detailed set of objectives to be realised. These have the potential to make a greater impact in terms of research deliverables, and the consequent benefits that can be brought to wider society.

Funding for research is increasingly competitive both nationally and internationally, so there is increasing emphasis on research quality. Thus individuals, research groups, and institutions, often seek to optimise their research strategies and research strengths in order to have maximum effect on their opportunities to support quality research, attract research grants, deliver research results, and attract other good researchers, whether academic staff or postgraduate students. The days of the individual researcher working in isolation are decreasing, unless this is done on a private basis, simply because the framework within which academic research is done has a greater degree of organisation, formalisation, accountability, and compliance due to the need to make the best use of limited resources. This framework typically seeks to synchronise its objectives with those of the funding agencies to maximise the chances of successful bids. In addition, those individuals who are involved in creative works such as painting or sculpture with associated exhibitions can often be incorporated into appropriate research groups, and may often obtain external sponsorship to support their work.

Keywords Corporate strategy • Research quality • Research impact • Research and innovation • Interdisciplinarity • Practice-based research • Practice-led research

1.1 Introduction

Many art schools were historically separate from Universities, having their own heritage, traditions and culture. The academic programmes were in many cases staffed by practitioners in the field who took on teaching in adjunct, part-time, roles. In recent years, many art schools have joined with their local Universities in order to benefit from marketing support, regulatory frameworks, student recruitment, and support for PhD students. This has brought them within the over-arching corporate strategies of these Universities, including their strategies for research. There were advantages to both parties in these mergers. The Universities benefited from a broader academic base and opportunities to further develop and advance interdisciplinary work. The art schools gained from the academic infrastructure, participation in quality assurance processes (such as academic standards and enhancement), opportunities to utilize technology, and access to computers and specialized equipment such as that used for imaging and stereolithography. More than this, however, the inevitable intermingling of differing subject specialisms in the academy has frequently generated previously-unsuspected interdisciplinary collaborations, for instance with computer science specialists in the digital media arena, with medical and health-related academics in explorations of therapies and the psychology of aesthetics, and with engineers in the use of advanced technologies to step beyond the traditional realms of 2D graphics and static sculptures.

Synchronizing with the University's research strategy has brought associated benefits in research support, staff training, collaboration with industry and commerce, and support for obtaining grants. However, it has also brought challenges and tensions due to the different kinds of research that characterise art and design. For example, practice–related research is an integral part of art and design but less common in other areas of the academy.

1.2 Research in Art and Design

Frayling [1] distinguished three distinct kinds of research in art and design: research *into* art and design, research *through* art and design, and research *for* art and design.

1.3 The UK Research Excellence Framework 2014   3

Research *into* art and design may include the following –

- Historical research
- Aesthetic or perceptual research
- Research into theoretical perspectives such as social, ethical, and cultural factors

Research *through* art and design may involve –

- Materials research such as that involved in pigments, metalwork, ceramics, and jewellery
- Development work – such as using a device in a new way
- Action research – a write-up of experimental practical work in a studio, including any design considerations which preceded the setup of the experiments

This can lead to a degree with the outputs verified mainly by project work, whether at undergraduate or postgraduate level.

Research in art and design involves the knowledge and understanding associated with creative works. Practice-led research is also an integral part of art and design. All these areas have been subject to ongoing discussion and debate.

Research *for* art and design may include the gathering of research materials, and the production of an artefact. This may include –

- The visual exhibition and communication of artefacts
- The cognitive tradition in fine art
- The expressive outcomes

This area is less easy to evaluate in terms of possible academic outcomes and deliverables, and is the subject of ongoing discussion.

Exhibitions, books, films, videos and broadcast media productions, and are more common as outputs rather than journals as in science and engineering, though research monographs are often used.

1.3 The UK Research Excellence Framework 2014

A further way to understand how research in art and design should be defined and developed is to analyse how the research audit process evaluated the research that has been completed in these areas over the previous 6 years in the UK.

The measurement of research quality performed in REF2014 [?] had three primary criteria – originality, significance and rigour. In general, these are accepted internationally as key measures of research excellence. They also broadly followed the criteria used in the national audit in 2008, with the additional criterion of impact. As the results of these measurements have implications for the ongoing research funding of institutions, the latter inevitably take substantial account of the kinds of research that are regarded as valid and also their objectives. These are set out in the REF2014 Panel Criteria and Working Methods [2]. The detail for art and design is set out in Part 2D Main Panel D Criteria, Unit of Assessment (UoA) 34. The following extract indicates the general approach that is taken [2].

UOA 34: Art and Design: History, Practice and Theory

24. The UOA includes research from all aspects of the history, theory and practice of art and design. The sub-panel will consider outputs, in whatever genre or medium, that meet the definition of research (as outlined in 'guidance on submissions', Annex C). The sub-panel acknowledges the diversity and range of related methods of academic study and artistic practice, and therefore adopts an inclusive definition of its remit.

25. **Practice** *encompasses all disciplines within art and design, in which methods of making, representation, interrogation and interpretation are integral to their productions.* **History** *and* **Theory** *encompass the history, criticism, theory, historiography, pedagogy and aesthetics of architecture, art, craft, and design in their widest chronological and geographical framework. The UOA may also embrace fields such as anthropology, archaeology, cultural, social and gender studies, entrepreneurship, innovation, management and business studies, media studies, museology, and urban planning, where these relate to visual, material and spatial cultures. In a number of cases, the fields of work may be interdisciplinary, and thus have no firm or rigidly definable boundaries. For this reason the subpanel expects to assess submissions that do not necessarily map onto institutional structures. The subpanel is committed to applying criteria and working methods that are appropriate to all submitting units, whatever their size or structure, without privileging any particular form of research output or environment.*

26. The following is an illustrative list of subject areas within practice, theory and history of art and design that the sub-panel expects to assess: animation; applied and decorative arts; architecture; conservation, the study of materials and techniques; crafts; creative and heritage industries; critical, historical, social and cultural studies; entrepreneurship and enterprise; film and broadcast media; fine arts; landscape and garden design; museology and curatorship; photography; policy, management and innovation studies; product design; spatial, two- and three-dimensional design; textile, dress and fashion; time-based and digital media; visual and material culture

In addition, a further section of this document outlines the way in which interdisciplinary research was included. Thus an area of art and design could combine with any other discipline in the REF2014 audit and be evaluated fairly using the contributions that each of the disciplines made in the research. This was done by cross-referencing these areas across the relevant sub-panels. In this sense, the terms of reference are quite open with regard to disciplines, since the objective is to allow new areas of research to grow and develop.

The assessment criteria focussed on research outputs (65 %), the impact of the research (20 %) and the environment in which the work was done (15 %). Outputs could include (but were not limited to) the following [2] –

- books (authored or edited)
- chapters in books
- Journal articles
- working papers
- published conference papers

- electronic resources and publications
- exhibition or museum catalogues
- translations; scholarly editions
- creative writing and compositions
- curatorship and conservation
- databases
- grammars
- dictionaries
- digital and broadcast media
- performances and other types of live presentation
- artefacts
- designs and exhibitions
- films, videos and other types of media presentation
- software design and development
- advisory report
- the creation of archival or specialist collections to support the research infrastructure.

In addition, all types of research or forms of output, whether they were physical or virtual, textual or non-textual, visual or sonic, static or dynamic, digital or analogue, were all equally acceptable and none had any advantage over the other.

In accepting this wide range of research types, the assessment methodologies were appropriate to all of these outputs and judged them entirely on research quality. No output was privileged or disadvantaged on the basis of the publisher, where it was published, or the medium of its publication [2].

Further information on how the research audit was performed is contained in Chap. 5.

The REF2014 audit produced a detailed report [3] after the analysis of all the submissions. This highlighted the following points –

1. This Unit of Assessment combined the areas of art and design. It identified a large amount of world-leading research and also confirmed the cognate nature of these two areas
2. There were significant achievements in the impact of the work
3. This Unit of Assessment had the largest amount of research through practice, and as such played a significant part in emergent approaches to the generation of knowledge
4. Interdisciplinary research is an innovative and productive part of the sector. For example, there are connections between the arts and the sciences, and also history and theory with current museums and galleries
5. Many of the research environments are capable of supporting world class research in art and design

However, there were some shortcomings in the quality of the portfolios for art and design.

1.4 Strategy in the European Union and National Science Foundation

National initiatives in the USA and many European countries are recognizing the benefits to scientific research in supporting larger groupings, often with interdisciplinary teams of researchers. It is possible to achieve results with a national grouping that it is not possible to achieve on the same time scale with an institutional one. This model has also been used for a number of years by the European Commission to facilitate research and innovation in European countries, and accomplish faster technology transfer to European industry by collaborators participating in projects. These initiatives have been extended to include non-European partners on a self-funded basis. Collaborative links have also been established with other countries. It is clear that with the increasing globalization of research and development there is a need for creative products that are competitive in world markets in order to remain viable.

The European Union's (EU) Research and Innovation Programme implements its policies in this domain [4]. These centre on converting innovative ideas into successful new products, technologies, and services. They seek to improve Europe's competitiveness, boost growth and create jobs. Research and innovation also help to make people's lives better by improving healthcare, transport, digital services and many new products and services requiring creative approaches. The innovation union is part of the Europe 2020 strategy, the EU's growth strategy, which stipulates an investment of 3 % of gross domestic product (GDP) in research and innovation, across the public and private sectors combined, by 2020. The EU's research framework programme, Horizon 2020, seeks to strengthen Europe's innovation leadership by fostering excellence in research and the development of innovative technologies. Approximately €80 billion is being invested in the period 2014–2020 in research and innovation projects. In the evaluation of research and innovation proposals, it uses three criteria [5] –

1. Excellence
2. Impact
3. Quality and efficiency of the implementation

In general, the excellence of a proposal is measured by the extent to which the proposed work is ambitious, has innovation potential, and goes beyond the state of the art (e.g. contains ground-breaking objectives, novel concepts and approaches). Evaluation is done by peer review by experts in the field. Evaluation scores out of 5 points are awarded for each of the criteria. The threshold for individual criteria is 3. The overall threshold, applying to the sum of the three individual scores, is 10. Proposals are ranked on the total score out of 15 and funding allocated in this order.

The European Research Council supports the highest quality research. It is driven by those who submit proposals which are evaluated on the basis of scientific excellence by peer review. Excellence is the sole criterion.

By way of comparison, the National Science Foundation, responsible for the funding of science and engineering research in the USA, had an annual budget in 2014 of $7.2 billion. In the evaluation of research proposals it uses two criteria –

1. Intellectual merit (meaning the potential to advance knowledge)
2. Broader impacts (encompassing the potential to benefit society and contributing to achieving specific, desired societal outcomes) [6]

Evaluation is done by peer review by experts in the field.

Thus the strategies for funding research are broadly similar, and focus on clear and demonstrable extension of current knowledge in the field, with coherent plans to migrate the outcomes of the work into new products and benefits for society. That is, the importance and significance of the work proposed is validated by demonstrating it advances the state of the art, and is relevant to the needs and requirements of society both nationally and internationally. These strategies and criteria also correlate well with those used for the audit and evaluation of research in the UK by REF2014 (see Sect. 1.3).

1.5 Strategy in the UK Research Councils

The UK Research Councils comprise the following –

- Arts & Humanities Research Council (AHRC)
- Biotechnology & Biological Sciences Research Council (BBSRC)
- Economic & Social Research Council (ESRC)
- Engineering & Physical Sciences Research Council (EPSRC)
- Medical Research Council (MRC)
- Natural Environment Research Council (NERC)
- Science & Technology Facilities Council (STFC)

The Research Councils UK body (RCUK) states the following with regard to its international strategy [7] –

> *The importance of co-ordinated international effort in changing views and delivering solutions to grand environmental and societal challenges is gaining greater global recognition, and continues to be a part of RCUK activities.*
> *RCUK will:*
>
> - *Address key global challenges using research as a driving force for change*
>   *RCUK supported research often has major consequences beyond national boundaries, bringing both direct and indirect national benefits, and influencing decision making at the highest levels.*
>
>   *As we implement current priority programmes and develop future priorities, we recognise the broader context of these programmes in shaping international agendas and addressing grand challenges.*

- *Promote the use of research to provide underpinning evidence for sound policy development*
  The acceleration of globalisation and environmental change has significant impact on individuals, the economy and society. Governments and international organisations will need to make far-reaching decisions in the coming decades. To make the right informed decisions they need the best available evidence, based on excellent research.
- **Work with others to recognise the value of international collaboration in building good relationships and improving understanding between nations**
  Relationships fostered in research partnerships contribute to enhanced mutual understanding, improving wider collaboration and security across international borders. RCUK optimises these benefits by working with others including the Foreign and Commonwealth Office and the Government's Science and Innovation Network.

The RCUK International Strategy recognises the value of research findings, in addressing key global issues such as poverty, disease, hunger, environmental degradation and security, and helping to inform policy solutions"

The strategy aims to -

- Increase RCUK influence in international research strategy and policy development
- Provide opportunities for excellent UK researchers to flourish in global research collaborations
- Enhance the value and impact of research through international collaboration
- Show RCUK commitment to key global responsibilities in a world where challenges cross national boundaries

The Councils have identified priority areas for research funding in order to address what are perceived to be the major problems confronting global society over the next 20 years. These are termed *"Grand Challenges"* and normally require multidisciplinary approaches on a national and international basis, and large-scale research projects in order to address them. These also seek to maximise domestic and international impact. These areas are as follows -

- Digital economy
- Energy
- Global food security
- Global uncertainties; security for all in a changing world
- Living with environmental change
- Lifelong health and wellbeing

All these areas have significant potential for delivering economic impact, as well as people with the right kinds of skills to carry the work forward. Although the themes declared above are very instrumental and utilitarian, they are intended to be wide-ranging and interdisciplinary and there is scope for inputs from art & design professionals under all of the headings.

Innovation UK (formerly the Technology Strategy Board) is also seeking to prioritise its work areas. Examples of these include the development of Innovation

Platforms, such as the Stratified Medicine *Innovation Platform, the* Sustainable Agriculture and Food *Innovation Platform, and the* Assisted Living *Innovation Platform.*

1.6 Strategy in the UK Arts and Humanities Research Council

The remit for the Arts and Humanities Research Council Strategy 2013–2018 includes the following statement –

Arts and humanities research changes the ways in which we see the world – the past world, the present world and the world of the future. It enhances understanding of our times, our capacities and our inheritance [8]

It explores forms of identity, behaviour and expression, and seeks out new ways of knowing what it means to be human in different societies and across the centuries. [8]

The AHRC Research Strategy 2013–2018 includes the following elements [8] –

- *The UK is a world leader in arts and humanities research. Over the next five years the AHRC will enhance our global distinction by focusing on excellence of achievement, extending opportunity and building capacity through partnerships.*
- *The AHRC will support cross-Council, cross-organisational and cross-disciplinary research to address complex problems and potentially transformative interdisciplinary work.*

Priorities include the supporting of the best project proposals, and to enable larger projects, including facilitating collaboration and interdisciplinarity. The best projects are those of highest quality and greatest ambition. Such project proposals are identified by peer review by experts in the field.

The AHRC also recognises that *"the international environment is highly competitive, requiring careful responses from the UK to retain its world-leading authority and an awareness that national research is inextricably international in both subject matter and use"* [8].

1.7 National Endowment for Science, Technology and the Arts (NESTA)

NESTA is committed to the development of partnerships and supporting innovation. This involves the creation and use of new ideas. It works across a broad range of sectors including digital arts and media, creative industries, health and ageing, citizen engagement in public services, government innovation, impact investment, innovation policy, new models for inclusive economic growth, opportunities for young people, and future thinking [9]. Nesta benefited from a £250 million endowment from the UK National Lottery. Investment interest earned by this fund is used to fund projects.

1.8 Current Research Strategies in Universities

The UK Research Assessment Exercise 2008 (RAE2008) defined research as –

Original investigation undertaken in order to gain knowledge and understanding. It includes work of direct relevance to the needs of commerce, industry, and to the public and voluntary sectors; scholarship[1]; the invention and generation of ideas, images, performances, artefacts including design, where these lead to new or substantially improved insights; and the use of existing knowledge in experimental development to produce new or substantially improved materials, devices, products and processes, including design and construction. It excludes routine testing and routine analysis of materials, components and processes such as for the maintenance of national standards, as distinct from the development of new analytical techniques. It also excludes the development of teaching materials that do not embody original research. [10]

The research strategies of universities in the UK generally focus on generating the highest quality research outputs and ensuring that such outputs (where relevant) have an appropriate impact on the external world that is recognised and valued. To produce such outputs generally requires research innovation and research collaborations.

Research strategies within Universities generally contain many of the following components, often with targets in the various areas over specific time periods –

- Refereed publications in journals, conferences, research monographs, and other outputs
- Acquisition of research grants
- PhD students, and postdoctoral research fellows
- Research collaborations – within the institution, regionally, nationally and internationally
- Developing research at the interface between disciplines and developing novel solutions
- Collaboration with industry – to facilitate industrial grants and knowledge transfer
- Ensuring research and innovation support services are efficient, effective and appropriate
- Ensuring new and emerging areas of research are supported and developed
- Ensuring compliance with relevant ethical requirements (e.g. with personal data)

---

[1]*Scholarship for the RAE is defined as "the creation, development and maintenance of the intellectual infrastructure of subjects and disciplines, in forms such as dictionaries, scholarly editions, catalogues and contributions to major research databases"* [10].

1.8 Current Research Strategies in Universities

- Mentoring framework to give support to new faculty and those with less experience
- Monitoring and planning cycles – to ensure continued delivery to the targets
- Informing the teaching programme of the institution, particularly at postgraduate level
- Compliance with regulatory frameworks such as those relating to open access to research outputs and research data
- Career development for researchers at all levels

Such environments also provide the opportunity for research students to make significant contributions to the work and receive appropriate training in research methods.

A PhD thesis must make an original contribution to knowledge. This is defined by the UK Quality Assurance Agency (QAA) as follows [11] -

Doctoral degrees are awarded to students who have demonstrated:

- *the creation and interpretation of new knowledge, through original research or other advanced scholarship, of a quality to satisfy peer review, extend the forefront of the discipline, and merit publication*
- *a systematic acquisition and understanding of a substantial body of knowledge that is at the forefront of an academic discipline or area of professional practice*
- *the general ability to conceptualise, design and implement a project for the generation of new knowledge, applications or understanding at the forefront of the discipline, and to adjust the project design in the light of unforeseen problems*
- *a detailed understanding of applicable techniques for research and advanced academic enquiry*

Research degrees in art and design incorporate the traditional approaches to the advancement of knowledge by published work. However, they also include practice-related research, of which there are two types -

1. In practice-based research the creative artefact or work is the primary focus of the contribution to knowledge
2. In practice-led research new understandings about the practice are the primary focus

The QAA summarised the situation with regard to such degrees in the UK as follows [12] -

The main characteristics of professional and practice-based doctorates are as follows.

Professional and practice-based doctorates usually contain taught elements with significant lecture and seminar content, but final award of the doctorate is based on a supervised research project, projects or portfolio. In some programmes, the taught elements are assessed and either a pass/fail, or a mark or grade, is given. Such assessments may act as incremental hurdles for the candidate as part of his/her progress towards the independent research project.

Research projects in professional doctorates are normally located within the candidate's profession or practice. In practice-based or practitioner doctorates the candidate's output involves practice-related materials. For example, in the performing arts, the output involves a written component, which complements the practice-based element (this may be shorter than the traditional PhD thesis, and includes both reflection and context), and one or more other artefacts, such as a novel (for creative writing), a portfolio of work (for art and design), or one or more performance pieces (for theatre studies, dance or music). In clinical practice-based doctorates, such as the DClinPsy or the MD, the research is likely to draw on clinical work involving clinical trials or other work with patients in the practical/clinical setting; the clinically based and academic research are then combined in the candidate's thesis or portfolio.

Professional doctorates are rooted in an academic discipline as well as in a profession (education, engineering, law and so on). Candidates whose research arises out of practice alone, who are not working in an academically related professional field and who spend most of their time learning in their work environment rather than with the higher education provider would be more likely to complete a practice-based doctorate. In both practice-based and professional doctorate settings, the candidate's research may result directly in organisational or policy-related change

With regard to the assessment and examination of the research work, the QAA states [12] -

As for the subject specialist study doctorate, professional and practice-based doctorates are assessed through submission of a thesis or portfolio, and in the vast majority of cases an individual oral examination ('viva' or 'viva voce'). The provider's definition of whether the award is a professional or practice-based doctorate will have a bearing on the assessment criteria for the degree. In the assessment of professional and/or practice-based doctorates, similar to the PhD, examiners' criteria may include the extent to which the candidate understands current techniques in the subject, for example through demonstrating engagement with and use of research methods and how they inform professional practice.

In the case of professional doctorates, successful completion of the degree normally leads to professional and/or organisational change that is often direct rather than achieved through the implementation of subsequent research findings

1.9 Increasing Selectivity in Research and Research Funding

The so-called "Golden Triangle" of British research-intensive Universities, Cambridge-Oxford-London [13] already received a large proportion of the total research funding in the UK via grants and the Quality Related (QR) funding from the Higher Education Funding Council for England (HEFCE). In 2010, HEFCE altered the QR funding formula to give a greater weighting to the highest ranked research (4*) [14]. This resulted in an additional £5 million Quality Related (QR) annual income to Oxford and Cambridge. The funding ratio in the model for "world-leading" (4*), "internationally excellent" (3*), and "recognised internationally" (2*) work was changed to 1:3:9, compared to the previous formula of 1:3:7. As shown in Table 1.1, the total percentage increase due to the change in funding formula in 2010 for the four Universities in the table was 10.9 %. The total research funding allocated to all Higher Education Institutions (HEIs) in 2015–2016 was £1.6 billion [15]. The four Universities listed received 30.2 % of the total. This is a significant proportion of the total funding and is also increasing over time. This has the effect of increasing the available resources for research in the high ranking Universities and therefore decreasing that in other Universities. Inclusion of Kings College London

1.10 Large Scale Collaborative Research Versus Individual Research

Table 1.1 Increases in funding for Universities in the Golden Triangle

Institution	Increase in funding (£)	Percentage increase	Total QR research funding 2015–2016	% of the total for all HEIs
University of Cambridge	2779 K	3.7	124,372 K	7.7
University of Oxford	2420 K	3.2	136,670 K	8.5
University College London	1335 K	2.2	124,888 K	7.8
Imperial College	907 K	1.8	99,059 K	6.2
Total	74,410 K	10.9	1,600,000 K all HEIs	30.2

and the London School of Economics into the grouping would increase the overall relative proportion by a further substantial amount.

The ranking of Universities uses national [16] and world league tables [17, 18]. Four national rankings of universities in the United Kingdom are published annually – by The Complete University Guide, The Guardian and jointly by The Times and The Sunday Times. Three world ranking of Universities are published annually – the Academic Ranking of World Universities (Shanghai Ranking), the QS World University Rankings and the Times Higher Education World University Rankings. These all use a number of performance indicators to determine an overall rank, and all include research except the Guardian which is more oriented towards parameters associated with the learning and teaching environment [19].

All the universities in the table above occupy some of the highest positions in the league tables (apart from some differences between the tables). Thus the standing in research enables these institutions to attract the best faculty and the best grants, which in turn increases the relative proportion of QR at every research audit (currently every 5 years). This results in the top Universities drawing away from the others in the tables and strengthening their positions at national and international levels.

A similar situation appertains to the Ivy League Universities [20] in the USA and their associated league table positions, though they are less dependent on external grant funding as they all have significant internal endowment funds.

In the UK, a group of smaller and specialist institutions co-operate through the Consortium for Research Training, Excellence and Support to increase their opportunities to gain funding for collaborative project work.

1.10 Large Scale Collaborative Research Versus Individual Research

The overall effect of the national and international policies and strategies outlined in the previous sections is to steer research and research funding priorities in the direction of national and international priorities and large-scale projects. This in turn favours larger Universities with large research groups and well-established national and international collaborations with significant research track records.

Research seeking funding in the UK and the EU has normally to consider the potential impact of the work done and the economic benefits to society. This has resulted in applicants for UK Research Council grants being asked to include an impact summary in their grant applications, and also detail how an economic return may be secured. Concerns about this shift have been expressed by senior academics in both the sciences and the arts, including six Nobel laureates, 80 fellows of the Royal Society and over 3000 professors [21]. One possible implication of the shift is that it could undermine support for basic research across all disciplines. In addition, the history of science and technology indicates that significant developments have occurred throughout history when researchers are allowed the freedom to pursue an area wherever it may lead. One possible effect of the shift to include impact and economic benefit is to narrow down the timescale of the research and to concentrate on those aspects which can be demonstrated to have a more immediate benefit. Seeking to meet the immediate needs of the market could result in an agenda which is driven more by the market than by the innate and long term value of the research. This could result in sacrificing more long term research areas over time which could have been a greater benefit to society over a longer timeframe.

An additional knock-on effect is to question the value of arts and humanities research, especially in those areas where it is difficult to clearly demonstrate immediate impact or economic benefit. The Council for the Defence of British Universities has argued the case that these policies imply a shift in the role of higher education institutions from knowledge discovery to *"the instrumentalisation of knowledge and its production"*. It also puts the case that *"the processes that underpin all education and knowledge are necessarily unpredictable and open-ended. So the universities that support those processes must be maintained as autonomous institutions to protect them"* [22].

The value of the arts and culture to society has therefore been repeatedly emphasised by leading scholars in the field and also by the UK Arts Council [23] and the American Academy of Arts and Sciences [24]. The case has also been made for a reconsideration of what is meant by 'value' where the term has come to be understood as principally synonymous with impact, or economic benefit, or making the case for public funding [25, 26]. It is recognised by national bodies that in times of economic recession or financial austerity then the arts and humanities come under attack [24, 27–29], and their value and merit need to be restated and reasserted.

In art and design, there are numerous areas where the output medium is an art work, an exhibition, or a monograph, rather than a journal or conference publication. In addition, there are many areas in art and design where there is potential for added-value research in collaboration with other disciplines. For example, Nesta's priority for proposals incorporating partnerships and innovation, gives a significant opportunity for multidisciplinary proposals to be funded. In addition, there is increasing recognition across all the UK Research Councils and the European Union research programmes of the importance and significance of multidisciplinary partnerships.

Multidisciplinary research is increasingly being recognised as an important component of research and development. Nobel laureate Sir Harry Kroto, president of the UK's Royal Society of Chemistry, advocates this approach – *"the traditional chemistry/physics/biology departmentalised university infrastructures – which are now clearly out-of-date and a serious hindrance to progress – must be replaced by new ones which actively foster the synergy inherent in multidisciplinarity"* [30]. Professional bodies are increasingly recognising the importance of including wider interdisciplinary aspects in the curricula of undergraduate degree programmes, in order to increase the basic knowledge base in this area and foster interdisciplinary thinking at the early stages in the understanding of a discipline. Mathematics and computer science are playing an increasingly important role at the interface with the life sciences in areas such as complex data analysis, manipulation and presentation, as well as modelling and simulation. They also assist in the traditional areas of science and engineering for analysis, modelling, and simulation. Art is playing an increasing role in the development of treatment therapies [31, 32]. It is important therefore that multidisciplinary aspects be incorporated into research strategies.

1.11 Conclusions

The rankings of higher education institutions in league tables are based on a range of performance indicators, normally including research [16, 17]. The position in the league tables can affect an institution's image and standing at national and international levels and its ability to attract the best students, grants, and faculty. Thus most institutions seek to improve their position in the league tables by improving their performance in line with the chosen criteria of the league table compilers. To improve research performance requires a research strategy which makes optimum use of an institution's strengths in order to be able to attract funding and deliver the research outputs that meet the criteria used to measure them.

There is increasing emphasis on research quality in order to meet the challenge of increasing research selectivity at national and international levels. Research funding is increasingly targeted at areas of national and international priority. Many of these areas require significant resources, expertise, and effort to address them. This implies major research groupings, often of a multidisciplinary nature, and across institutions at national and international levels.

Further Reading

General Books on Research and Development in Art and Design

Biggs, M., Karlsson, H. (eds.): Routledge Companion to Research in the Arts, p. 488. Routledge (2012)

Dunne, A., Raby, F.: Speculative Everything: Design, Fiction, and Social Dreaming, p. 200. MIT Press, Cambridge, MA (2014)

Munari, B.: Design as Art, p. 224. Penguin Classics, Baltimore (2008)

Nelson, R. (ed.): Practice as Research in the Arts: Principles, Protocols, Pedagogies, Resistances, p. 248. Palgrave Macmillan, Basingstoke (2013)
Yelavich, S., Adams, B.: Design as Future Making, p. 256. Bloomsbury Academic, London (2014)

General Books on Universities and University Strategy

Bowen, W.G.: Lessons Learned: Reflections of a University President, p. 184. Princeton University Press, Princeton (2013)
Brown, R.: Everything for Sale? The Marketisation of UK Higher Education, p. 256. Routledge (2013)
Bushaway, R.: Managing Research, p. 264. Open University Press, Maidenhead (2003)
Clark, B.R.: Creating Entrepreneurial Universities: Organizational Pathways of Transformation, p. 180. Pergamon, Oxford (1998)
Cole, J.R.: The Great American University: Its Rise to Pre-eminence, Its Indispensable National Role, Why It Must Be Protected, p. 640. Public Affairs US (2012)
Collini, S.: What Are Universities for? p. 240. Penguin, London (2012)
McGettigan, A.: The Great University Gamble: Money, Markets, and the Future of Higher Education, p. 232. Pluto Press, London (2013)
Palfreyman, D., Tapper, T.: Re-Shaping the University: The Rise of the Regulated Market in Higher Education, p. 336. OUP, Oxford (2014)
Shattock, M.: Entrepreneurialism in Universities and the Knowledge Economy: Diversification and Organizational Change in European Higher Education, p. 256. Open University Press, Maidenhead (2008)
Shattock, M.: Managing Successful Universities, p. 240. Open University Press, Maidenhead (2010)
Watson, D.: Managing Strategy, p. 176. Open University Press, Buckingham (2000)
Watson, D.: The Question of Morale: Managing Happiness and Unhappiness in University Life, p. 165. Open University Press, Maidenhead (2009)

References

1. Frayling, C.: Research in Art and Design, Royal College of Art. http://www.transart.org/wp-content/uploads/group-documents/79/1372332724-Frayling_Research-in-Art-and-Design.pdf (1994)
2. REF2014 panel criteria and working methods. http://www.ref.ac.uk/pubs/2012-01/
3. REF2014: overview report by main panel D and sub-panels 27 to 36. http://www.ref.ac.uk/media/ref/content/expanel/member/Main%20Panel%20D%20overview%20report.pdf (Jan 2015)
4. Research and Innovation – European Commission. http://europa.eu/pol/pdf/flipbook/en/research_en.pdf, http://europa.eu/pol/index_en.htm, http://europa.eu/!bY34KD
5. Horizon – work programme 2014–2015 – General Annexes H2020 evaluation. http://ec.europa.eu/research/participants/data/ref/h2020/wp/2014_2015/annexes/h2020-wp1415-annex-h-esacrit_en.pdf
6. NSF strategic plan for 2014-18 http://www.nsf.gov/pubs/2014/nsf14043/nsf14043.pdf
7. Our Vision for International Collaboration. Research Councils UK. http://www.rcuk.ac.uk/RCUK-prod/assets/documents/publications/international.pdf
8. Arts and Humanities Research Council strategy 2013-18. http://www.ahrc.ac.uk/documents/publications/the-human-world-the-arts-and-humanities-in-our-times-ahrc-strategy-2013-2018/
9. NESTA strategy for 2014-17. http://www.ncsta.org.uk/publications/nesta-strategy-2014-2017
10. Research Assessment Exercise (RAE). www.rae.ac.uk/pubs/2005/03/rae0305.doc (2008)

References

11. The UK doctorate: a guide for current and prospective doctoral candidates, QAA. http://www.qaa.ac.uk/en/Publications/Documents/Doctorate-guide.pdf (2011)
12. Doctoral degree characteristics statement, QAA. http://www.qaa.ac.uk/en/Publications/Documents/Doctoral-Degree-Characteristics-15.pdf (Sept 2015)
13. Golden Triangle of Universities. https://en.wikipedia.org/wiki/Golden_triangle_%28universities%29
14. Golden Triangle to win funding riches, Times Higher. https://www.timeshighereducation.com/news/golden-triangle-to-win-funding-riches/410357.article (11 Feb 2010)
15. HEFCE funding of teaching and research 2015-16. http://www.hefce.ac.uk/pubs/year/2015/201506/
16. Rankings of universities in the UK. https://en.wikipedia.org/wiki/Rankings_of_universities_in_the_United_Kingdom
17. Academic ranking of world universities. https://en.wikipedia.org/wiki/Academic_Ranking_of_World_Universities
18. The world's most international universities, Times Higher. https://www.timeshighereducation.com/features/200-most-international-universities-world-2016 (14 Jan 2016)
19. Education Guardian University league tables. http://www.theguardian.com/education/ng-interactive/2015/may/25/university-league-tables-2016 (2016)
20. Ivy league universities. https://en.wikipedia.org/wiki/Ivy_League
21. UCU – the research excellence framework. http://www.ucu.org.uk/index.cfm?articleid=4207 (2013)
22. Council for the Defence of British Universities. http://cdbu.org.uk/
23. The Value of Arts and Culture to People and Society. The Arts Council. http://www.artscouncil.org.uk/media/uploads/pdf/The-value-of-arts-and-culture-to-people-and-society-An-evidence-review-Mar-2014.pdf
24. Rosen, A: Liberal arts, British style. Times Higher. https://www.timeshighereducation.com/comment/opinion/liberal-arts-british-style/2005765.article (18 July 2013)
25. Belfiore, E.: 'Impact', 'value' and 'bad economics': making sense of the problem of value in the arts and humanities. Arts Humanit. High. Educ. **14**(1), 95–110 (2015). ISSN 1474-0222
26. Donovan, C.: Creating #havoc: A holistic approach to valuing our culture. In: Powell, A., Swindells, S. (eds.) "What is to be Done?": Cultural Leadership and Public Engagement in Art and Design Education", Cambridge Scholars Publishing. http://www.cambridgescholars.com/download/sample/61702, http://eprints.hud.ac.uk/19803/3/Symposium_pack.pdf (2014)
27. Eastwood D. Two tribes? Science and art are more alike than unalike, Times Higher. https://www.timeshighereducation.com/comment/opinion/two-tribes-science-and-art-are-more-like-than-unalike/2019156.article (19 Mar 2015)
28. Kleiman, P.: Arts education: banished beyond the debatable hills? Times Higher. https://www.timeshighereducation.com/blog/arts-education-banished-beyond-debatable-hills (27 Dec 2015)
29. Blackburn, S., Alessandri, M., Kaag, J.: Can philosophy survive in an academy driven by impact and employability? Times Higher. https://www.timeshighereducation.com/features/can-philosophy-survive-in-an-academy-driven-by-impact-and-employability (10 Dec 2015)
30. Toni, B. (ed): New Frontiers of Multidisciplinary Research in STEAM-H. Springer (2014)
31. Earnshaw, R.A., Liggett, S., Heald, K.: Interdisciplinary Collaboration Methodologies in Art, Design and Media. Proceedings of International Conference on Internet Technologies and Applications, pp381-388, ISBN 978-0-946881-81-9, UK. Download PDF (2013)
32. Liggett, S., Heald, K., Earnshaw, R.A., Thompson, E., Excell, P.S.: Collaborative Research in Art, Design and New Media – Challenges and Opportunities, Proceedings of Internet Technologies and Applications, 2015. For more information see: http://ita15.net/ita-art-expo/ Download PDF

Chapter 2
Models for Research in Art, Design, and Creativity

Abstract Advancement of knowledge and understanding is a prerequisite for research in any discipline. This may be accomplished by models that are able to develop and advance the field, and provide a basis for critical analysis and reflection. Such models must also be relevant to the modes of analysis involved, and it is useful if they are also consistent with internal and external strategies for research, and the funding, evaluation, and audit of research. The implications of institutional and national measurements can often affect the advancement and promotion of academic staff, and the funding allocations to the institution as a consequence of national audit. This can become a virtuous circle and lead to greater research advances in the field than might have otherwise been possible.

Keywords Research models • Research development • Research assessment • Practice-led research • Interdisciplinary research

2.1 Introduction

One definition of research is *"the systematic investigation into, and study of, materials and sources in order to establish facts and reach new conclusions"* [1]. This results in the accumulation of knowledge and understanding about the areas being investigated. These can include humans, culture, society, and the physical world. The processes involved can confirm facts or establish new ones, solve problems, investigate a theory or develop new theories. Methodologies depend upon epistemologies which vary between sciences and the humanities. For example, the arts may use qualitative methods and critical analysis to arrive at conclusions, in contrast to the classical scientific methods which work more by experiment, testing hypotheses, and quantitative analysis.

A further definition of artistic research is as follows –

> Artistic research is to investigate and test with the purpose of gaining knowledge within and for our artistic disciplines. It is based on artistic practices, methods and criticality. Through presented documentation, the insights gained shall be placed in a context. [2]

Topal [3] comments on artistic research –

perhaps more so than other disciplines, intuition is utilized as a method to identify a wide range of new and unexpected productive modalities [3]

Schiesser [4] and Earnshaw et al. [5] comment on some of the current issues in artistic research.

As set out in Chap. 1, Frayling [6] distinguished three distinct kinds of research in art and design: research *into* art and design, research *through* art and design, and research *for* art and design.

The UK Arts and Humanities Research Council defines arts and humanities as follows -

Arts and humanities research changes the ways in which we see the world – the past world, the present world and the world of the future. It enhances understanding of our times, our capacities and our inheritance.

It explores forms of identity, behaviour and expression, and seeks out new ways of knowing what it means to be human in different societies and across the centuries. [7]

Books, films, videos, radio documentaries, and exhibition catalogues are more common as outputs rather than journals as in science and engineering, though journals are used as well.

2.2 Research in Art and Design

Research in the sciences is generally depicted as a process by which a hypothesis is tested and then refined until it is validated with a wide variety of data.

In order to define a model for art and design it is first necessary to consider how the research community perceives the nature and goals of research in this area. The REF2014 panel consisted of leading academics in the field with international representation. Their objective was to evaluate the quality of the research done in UK Universities by a process of peer review. Further detail on the process and outcomes is in Chap. 5. In order to evaluate the outcomes, the panel first needed to define the disciplines and their objectives.

The REF2014 Panel defined the disciplines comprising Art and Design in the Unit of Assessment 34 [5] as follows –

Practice encompasses all disciplines within art and design, in which methods of making, representation, interrogation and interpretation are integral to their productions. History and Theory encompass the history, criticism, theory, historiography, pedagogy and aesthetics of architecture, art, craft, and design in their widest chronological and geographical framework. The UOA may also embrace fields such as anthropology, archaeology, cultural, social and gender studies, entrepreneurship, innovation, management and business studies, media studies, museology, and urban planning, where these relate to visual, material and spatial cultures. In a number of cases, the fields of work may be interdisciplinary, and thus have no firm or rigidly definable boundaries. For this reason the sub- panel expects to assess submissions that do not necessarily map onto institutional structures. The sub-

2.2 Research in Art and Design

panel is committed to applying criteria and working methods that are appropriate to all submitting units, whatever their size or structure, without privileging any particular form of research output or environment.

26. The following is an illustrative list of subject areas within practice, theory and history of art and design that the sub-panel expects to assess: animation; applied and decorative arts; architecture; conservation, the study of materials and techniques; crafts; creative and heritage industries; critical, historical, social and cultural studies; entrepreneurship and enterprise; film and broadcast media; fine arts; landscape and garden design; museology and curatorship; photography; policy, management and innovation studies; product design; spatial, two- and three-dimensional design; textile, dress and fashion; time-based and digital media; visual and material culture [5]

More detail is provided in the definitions associated with Unit of Assessment (UOA) 34 in the REF2014 specification [8]: this has the formal title *"Art and Design: History, Practice and Theory"*.

Interdisciplinary research was addressed in the following way –

38. The main panel recognises that the UOAs described above do not have firm or rigidly definable boundaries, and that aspects of research are naturally interdisciplinary or multi-disciplinary or span the boundaries between individual UOAs, whether within the main panel or across main panels.

39. The arrangements for assessing interdisciplinary research and submissions that span UOA boundaries – including through the appointment of assessors and, where necessary, cross-referring specific parts of submissions between sub-panels – are common across all main panels and are described in Part 1, paragraphs 92–100.

40. In addition, Main Panel D recognises that there are research areas which may be undertaken in a range of different contexts, and some of these therefore occur in the descriptors of a number of UOAs. These areas include but are not limited to: applied linguistics, critical theory, cultural history, digital cultural heritage, digital humanities, film studies, gender studies, history of science and technology, television studies and museology. The main panel takes the view that institutions active in such areas are free to submit their research in the way that represents the activity most effectively. Panels' working methods will accommodate such instances [8]

The extent to which this procedure did full justice to the value of interdisciplinary research is not known as, apart from the formal published outputs of the panel, all discussions within it were confidential. However, it has been observed that although obtaining the view of an expert in another discipline within interdisciplinary research could result in an evaluation of that component of the work, it may not do full justice to the combined work. For example, the extent to which the combined work yielded more than the sum of the component parts is a key aspect of interdisciplinary research, i.e. the degree to which each discipline in the collaboration added value to the other(s). It is not clear whether this aspect has been fully recognised, or what methods may have been used to measure this.

Science and technology are increasingly providing tools and facilities as components of the environments where art works are produced, and are also in some case integral parts of the works that are created. In the area of creative industries, technology often becomes a component of the implementation and delivery platforms. By definition, digital media outputs are based on digital technology. However, it is the creative content which is the key to its value and impact. Thus the creative skills in art and design are essential components of the work. Thus art and design can make very valuable contributions to the creative enterprise.

In the research evaluation of RAE2008, the Art and Design Panel issued an overview report [9] of the evaluation which included the following –

14) There were a large number of outputs characterised by interdisciplinary practice, artist/curator projects and collaborations, installation, moving image, lens- and text-based work. At its best, the fine art submitted for assessment displayed an understanding of the contextual framework needed for a research assessment exercise, with a depth of evidence and corroborating material that helped present the research in the round. Research, however, is not always a rhetorical enterprise and the sub-panel identified strong work that showed systematic enquiry, critical reflection, and appropriate means of dissemination. As with design, although the sub-panel saw evidence of strong work in all aspects of fine art, there was considerable variety in levels of scholarship and there remains a difficulty in accessing evidence of inquiry in some of the more traditional practices.

15) The sub-panel noted considerable examples of collaboration with science, especially in the fields of ecology and genetics, and there were distinct crossovers between fine art and design, architecture and the built environment. It is clear that enquiry into curatorial processes and histories has exponentially increased in the art and design sector during the assessment period, with a number of institutions pursuing curatorial research through their own individual and thematically directed research, post-graduate and cultural engagement programmes. The emphasis to date has been around contemporary art and site-specific curating, but in the future the sector could expect to see more work in design and built environment, especially in relation to audience, participation and interactivity, as well as the physical construction and organisation of exhibitions. The key challenges in the future will be to forge firmer and more innovative partnerships with the established museum and gallery sectors, to document and disseminate curatorial research more extensively, and to link with the conventional publishing and the new media sectors more meaningfully [6]

Thus there was clear evidence of interdisciplinary research and the expectation that this would develop further. This implies therefore that models and structures for art and design need to be able to support this, value it, and allow opportunity for expansion of existing collaborations, and also increase the range and diversity of the disciplines and the collaborations.

Quality profiles for Research Environment reveal that the majority of submissions contained high levels of achievement. The sub-panel was most impressed by narratives that included clearly described strategies and structures that were firmly embedded in the research culture and were linked to concrete detail. A number of institutions have made large-scale infrastructural and capital investments in art and design in recent years, and there are many cases where emergent departments had clearly benefited from strong, focused support at institutional level. In a few instances, however, institutional support seemed less certain, with a concomitant impact on research activity. [6]

In REF2014, the Art and Design Sub-Panel overview report [10] included the following -

The creation of this sub-panel has demonstrated a number of very positive things. First, a large amount of world-leading research is being conducted in numerous HEIs. Second, the ability of the art and design sector to convert research scored at 2* and above into outstanding and very considerable impact was impressive, and fully reveals the importance of the sector in UK and international society. "Third, art and design is the largest sector for the production of research through practice, and as such is a leader in the elaboration of *emergent approaches to knowledge. Fourth, the sector has become one of the most important for the development of innovative and productive interdisciplinary research. The connection of the arts with the sciences, and of history and theory with museums and galleries, to cite two examples, reveals the complex, dynamic and impactful condition of research in the sector. Fifth, the environment exists in abundance for the conducting of world class research in art and design.* [10]

Thus the quality of research and its impact are substantial, and there is substantial potential for the future. In addition, the importance of research through practice and interdisciplinary work is recognised.

2.3 Practice-Led Research

Practice-led/practitioner research in art is not always based on an external stimulus or problem. In fact, some research in art and design fits very comfortably within the Academic Research Model framework as depicted in Sect. 2.2.

An investigation into practice-led research in the fields of art, design and architecture was undertaken by the Arts and Humanities Research Council in the UK in 2007 [11]. This has informed the understanding of various aspects of research in this area. The starting point for practice-led research was as defined as follows –

The professional disciplines of art, design and architecture have many differences but all share a tradition of situating learning and scholarship in a professional practice setting. 'Practice-led research' can be thought of as a natural extension of this principle since many academics in these fields see practice as the natural arena for inquiry and the methods of practice as methods of inquiry. [11]

It was recognised by the review panel that these disciplines have some differences to the norm -

In particular we have come to the conclusion that conventional ideas of contribution to knowledge or understanding may not be serving us well. This is significant to fine artists but we believe that it relevant across ADA and a shared effort to develop appropriate new models would be a constructive development. [11]

This included the nature of the outputs –

The debate on validity of practice-led research tends to be dominated by the question of outputs, characterised by arguments about the admissibility of artefacts in place of conventional texts. While some of this debate is irrelevant and promoted by relatively inexperienced individuals, it does appear that the nature of output, or rather contribution, may be a core issue for Fine Art in particular but also for design and architecture to some degree. [11]

A key aspect of practice-led research is the definition of new knowledge. This may be defined as follows [12] –

Practice-based Research *is an original investigation undertaken in order to gain new knowledge partly by means of practice and the outcomes of that practice. Claims of originality and contribution to knowledge may be demonstrated through creative outcomes*

***Practice-led Research** is concerned with the nature of practice and leads to new knowledge that has operational significance for that practice. The main focus of the research is to advance knowledge about practice, or to advance knowledge within practice*

Sullivan discusses [13] how *"facing the unknown and disrupting the known is precisely what artist researchers achieve as they delve into theoretical, conceptual, dialectical and conceptual practices through artmaking"*. The search for, and impact on, new knowledge currently places responsibilities on the artist-researcher, challenging them to theorise their practice to self, others and communities. It is no longer possible for artist-researchers in academe to *"hide behind the role of the mute artist"* [14]. For practice-led researchers it is therefore no longer feasible to borrow methods from other disciplines as this denies artist researchers *"intellectual maturity of arts practice as a plausible basis for raising significant theoretical questions and as a viable site for undertaking important artistic, cultural and educational enquires"* [13].

The artist may be faced with a number of decisions to make and a number of approaches to take. This produces a process which is nondeterministic -

Artistic research can never be characterised by a well-defined, rigid methodology. Rather, its form of research could be described as a methodical: it entails a strong belief in a methodological articulable result founded by operational strategies that cannot be legitimized beforehand. Indeed, that is the essential characteristic of artistic research [15].

Innovative approaches may be devised if no current methodologies exist [16].

The recent trend to include a measurement of the effect of research in the UK outside the academy (termed 'impact') provides opportunities for art and design to utilise creative outputs to demonstrate cultural and economic value. This could be in terms of galleries and exhibitions, and other outreach activities undertaken by the artists. REF2014 defined impact as *"an effect on, change or benefit to the economy, society, culture, public policy or services, health, the environment or quality of life, beyond academia"*. [8, 17]

The Step-change for Higher Arts Research and Education (SHARE) network [18], supported by the European Commission, has advanced the agenda for artistic research by developing a collaborative network of partners. It has sought to demonstrate that it is possible to support *"a range of practices that have not been exhaustively predetermined and co-opted by the current fashions of art, intellect and policy, while negotiating a language of accountability of outcomes, outputs and metrics"* [19].

The field of architecture illustrates the significance and importance of innovation in design -

In architecture there is a long tradition in the UK of carrying out research in practice. Indeed to maintain a distinctive profile in the marketplace, it is almost a requirement for the most innovative practices to develop new ideas and methods through research. [11]

2.4 Models for Research in Art and Design

Defining knowledge is a challenging task and belongs more to the disciplines of philosophy and epistemology. However, a brief consideration is required in order to provide a starting point to a definition. Knowledge acquisition is generally regarded as having two traditions. The first, empiricism, states that knowledge is acquired from experience and observation of the world about us. The second, rationalism, states that knowledge is acquired by the application of reason alone. An example of the latter might be aesthetics, the nature of art, beauty, and taste, with the creation and appreciation of beauty. Empiricism requires that claims be tested in order to demonstrate whether they are true or not. This has led some to the position of radical empiricism, such as logical positivism, where abstract concepts such as religious or ethical claims are regarded as meaningless because no observations can confirm them. However, it is possible to take a middle ground in this debate where exceptions to the general rule are allowable. It is also possible to consider how far the two traditions may both be explored to ascertain how each is able to contribute to an understanding of a discipline. A priori knowledge is that which is known independently of experience and *a posteriori* knowledge is derived from experience.

Brown et al. [20] proposed four types of research in the creative arts and design –

(i) *Scholarly Research*
(ii) *Pure Research*
(iii) *Developmental Research*
(iv) *Applied Research*

These were summarised as follows by Brown et al. [20] –

Scholarly Research – creates and sustains the intellectual infrastructure within which Pure, Developmental and Applied research can be conducted. It aims to map the fields in which issues, problems, or questions are located (what is known or understood in the general area of the proposed research already, and how addressing or answering the issues, problems or questions specified will enhance the generally-available knowledge, and, understanding of the area in question).

Pure Research – asks fundamental questions in the field and explores hypotheses experimentally. It searches for pure knowledge that may uncover issues, theories, laws or metaphors that may help explain why things operate as they do, why they are as they are, or, why they appear to look the ways they do.

Developmental research – serves two purposes (a) it identifies the limitations of existing knowledge as evolved through Pure research by creating alternative models ... (b) it harnesses, tests and reworks existing knowledge so to evolve special methods, tools and resources in preparation for the solving of specific problems, in specific contexts, through Applied research.

Applied Research – involves a process of systematic investigation within a specific context in order to solve an identified problem in that context. It aims to create new or improved systems (of thought or production), artefacts, products, processes, materials, devices, or services for long-term economic, social and/or cultural benefit

Clarke identified two principal kinds of research model (or paradigm) based on Creswell [22, 23] –

1. *Quantitative* – traditional, positivist, experimental or empiricist – following Comte, Mill, Durkheim, Newton, Locke
2. *Qualitative* – constructivist, naturalistic, interpretive, postpositivist, postmodern – following Dithy, Kant, Wittgenstein, Foucault, Miles, Huberman

Clarke [21] argues that there are fundamental differences between these kinds of model as follows –

- *Nature of reality – ontology*
- *Relationship to that being researched – epistemology*
- *Role of values – axiology*
- *Use of language/words – rhetorical*
- *Overall process of research – methodological*

According to Clarke, research should provide –

- *A system of classification*
- *Offer explanations*
- *Make predictions*
- *Acquire a sense of understanding*

Rosenberg [24] advocates the "Poetic Model" of research where new ideas may be discontinuous with the old. This may be seen in contrast to the incremental model of knowledge advancement which proceeds on the basis of systematic and iterative development from the status quo, which is common in the sciences.

Hannula et al. [25] state the case for the advancement of artistic research by the production of art works, researching the creative process, and the accumulation of knowledge in the field built upon practice.

2.5 Models for Research in Creativity

Thomas et al. [26] summarise the range of theories, functions and practices associated creativity in a wide range of disciplines including art, creative industries, aesthetics, design, new media, music, arts education, science, engineering and technology.

Chapter 4 on Creativity has more detail on this aspect.

2.6 The Relationship of Art and Design to Technology

There are a number of aspects to the relationship of art and design to technology. These include the following –

(i) Technology support in art studios
(ii) Technology that provides new digital environments
(iii) Dissemination of art works via technology
(iv) Digital art

(i) Technology support in Art Studios: in the process of creating artworks

Technology, including computers and software, provides tools and facilities to augment the traditional art and design processes of creating. These can assist in the production of new art forms, for example David Hockney's production of artworks using the iPad [27].

(ii) Technology that provides new digital environments for the creative process

Various forms of technology have been utilised in art and design from computer screens to CAVEs – see Chap. 4 on Creativity for further information.

(iii) Dissemination of Artworks Via Virtual Museums and Art Galleries

The Internet can be utilised to provide ubiquitous and personalized experiences of artworks. Augmentation using social media can provide communal experiences of the artworks. This has raised the question of the extent to which physical museums and galleries can provide a fuller experience of the art works and how far this can be replicated in virtual environments.

(iv) Digital Art

Digital art is produced and presented using the medium of technology. Such art may be produced by simulations on computers. Visual effects in animations and films are often produced directly with software on computers rather than by filming physical models. Storytelling, theatre, and art have been used for centuries to create artificial worlds in the mind. Virtual reality and imaging techniques are further communication tools which can advance this process [28, 29].

Clark [30] argued that one Internet year is equivalent to seven calendar years, and therefore the more significant the Internet becomes, the faster the processes and developments associated with it will take place. Thus digital technologies can have a transformative effect on the field in a relatively short period of time.

2.7 Conclusions

Formalising research in art, design and creativity is a difficult challenge. They are a very broad set of disciplines comprising research *into* art and design, research *through* art and design, and research *for* art and design. At the same time, art and design are making increasing connections to other disciplines and are engaged in collaborative research projects. Interdisciplinary research may increase in the future, especially if new areas at the boundaries between disciplines are seen to bring significant new advances in knowledge and understanding. Technology is also becoming increasingly user-centred and pervasive, and can provide added value to the processes of art and design. Thus all frameworks and models in art and design need to be flexible and open-ended, whilst recognising the need to consider the parameters of research assessment and audit which determine standing, reputation, and funding.

Further Reading

Art Practices as Research. https://thinkingpractices.wordpress.com/theories-of-art-practices-as-research/

Bolter, J.D., Grusin, R.: Remediation: Understanding New Media, p. 312. MIT Press, Cambridge, MA (1998)

Freeland, C.: Art Theory: A Very Short Introduction. Oxford University Press, Oxford. Chapter 7 "Digitizing and Disseminating" (2001)

Glassner, A.: 3D Computer Graphics, A User's Guide for Artists and Designers, p. 214. Herbert Press (1991)

Gray, C., Malins, J.: Visualizing Research: A Guide to the Research Process in Art and Design. Ashgate, Aldershot (2004)

Gray, C., Malins, J.: Research Procedures and Methodologies for Artists and Designers.http://carolegray.net/Papers%20PDFs/epgad.pdf (1993)

HEFCE metrics workshop: metrics and the assessment of research quality and impact in the arts and humanities. http://www.hefce.ac.uk/news/events/2015/events99364.html (2015)

Innovate UK's creative industries strategy 2013–16. https://connect.innovateuk.org/documents/3220887/3676376/Creative%20Industries%20Strategy%202013-2016?version=1.0

Kwastek, K.: Aesthetics of Interaction in Digital Art, p. 384. MIT Press. https://mitpress.mit.edu/books/aesthetics-interaction-digital-art (2013)

Laurel, B.: Computers as Theatre, 2nd ed, p. 272. Addison-Wesley Professional, Upper Saddle River (2013)

Nesta: A Manifesto for the Creative Economy.http://www.nesta.org.uk (2013)

Seven Ways Technology Is Changing How Art Is Made. http://www.smithsonianmag.com/arts-culture/7-ways-technology-is-changing-how-art-is-made-180952472/?no-ist

Zurich University Dep of Art & Media (author, ed.), Brunner, C., Schiesser, G. (eds.): Practices of Experimentation. Research and Teaching in the Arts Today. Scheidegger & Spiess Verlag/Chicago: University Press 2012 (Co-editor), ISBN 978-3-85881-259-9

References

1. Oxford Dictionaries. http://www.oxforddictionaries.com/definition/english/research (2015)
2. Unattributed. Artistic research at DOCH. Dans och Cirkushögskolan (website). Retrieved 14 Aug 2011
3. Topal, H.: Whose Terms? A Glossary for Social Practice: RESEARCH (2014)
4. Schiesser, G.: What is at stake – Qu'est ce que l'enjeu? Paradoxes – Problematics – Perspectives in Artistic Research Today. In: Gerald, G., Carayannis, E.G., Campbell, D.F.J. (eds.) Arts, Research, Innovation and Society Series. pp. 197–210. Springer, Wien (2015)
5. Earnshaw, R.A., Liggett, S., Cunningham, S., Heald, K., Thompson, E.: Models for Research in Art, Design, and the Creative Industries. Proceedings of Internet Technologies and Applications. For more information see: http://ita15.net/ita-art-expo/DownloadPDF (2015)
6. Frayling, C.: Research in Art and Design. Royal College of Art. http://www.transart.org/wp-content/uploads/group-documents/79/1372332724-Frayling_Research-in-Art-and-Design.pdf (1994)
7. AHRC strategy, 2013–18. P 5 in http://www.ahrc.ac.uk/News-and-Events/News/Documents/AHRC-Strategy-2013-18.pdf
8. REF2014. Panel Criteria and Working Methods. http://www.ref.ac.uk/media/ref/content/pub/panelcriteriaandworkingmethods/01_12_2D.pdf (2012)
9. RAE2008. Panel Overview Reports. Points 14 and 18 (iv) for UoA 63 – http://www.rae.ac.uk/pubs/2009/ov/ (2008)
10. REF2014. Panel Overview Reports. Point 29 in UoA 34 -http://www.ref.ac.uk/media/ref/content/expanel/member/Main%20Panel%20D%20overview%20report.pdf (2015)
11. Practice-Led Research in Art, Design and Architecture – AHRC Review.https://ia802604.us.archive.org/11/items/ReviewOfPractice-ledResearchInArtDesignArchitecture/Pactice-ledReviewNov07.pdf (Nov 2007)
12. http://www.creativityandcognition.com/research/practice-based-research/differences-between-practice-based-and-practice-led-research/
13. Sullivan, G.: Making space. In: Smith, H., Dean, R.T. (eds.) Practice-Led Research, Research-Led Practice in the Creative Arts. Edinburgh University Press, Edinburgh (2009)
14. Mäkelä, M., Routarinne, S.: Connecting different practices. In: Mäkelä, M., Routarinne, S. (eds.) The Art of Research: Research Practices in Art and Design. University of Art and Design Helsinki, Finland (2006)
15. Slager, H.: Art and method. In: Elkins, J. (ed.) Artists with PhDs: On the New Doctoral Degree in Studio Art. New Academia Publishing, Washington, DC (2009)
16. Gray, C., Malins, J.: Visualising Research: A Guide to the Research Process in Art and Design. Ashgate Publishing Limited, Aldershot (2004)
17. REF2014. Assessment Criteria and Level Definitions. http://www.ref.ac.uk/panels/assessmentcriteriaandleveldefinitions/ (2014)
18. Step-Change for Higher Arts Research and Education (SHARE). http://www.sharenetwork.eu/
19. Wilson, M., Van Ruiten, S.: SHARE Handboook for Artistic Research Education. p. 2. http://www.sharenetwork.eu/resources/share-handbook (2013)
20. Brown, B., Gough, P., Roddis, J.: Types of Research in the Creative Arts and Design. Discussion paper. http://arts.brighton.ac.uk/__data/assets/pdf_file/0003/43077/4_research.pdf (2004)
21. Clarke, R.J.: Research Models and Methodologies.http://www.uow.edu.au/content/groups/public/@web/@commerce/documents/doc/uow012042.pdf, http://www.slideshare.net/eilire91/qualitative-vs-quantitative (2005)
22. Creswell, J.W.: Research Design: Qualitative, Quantitative and Mixed Method Approaches. Sage Publications, Thousand Oaks (2002)
23. Creswell, J.W.: A Concise Introduction to Mixed Methods Research. Sage, Los Angeles (2014)

24. Rosenberg, T.: The Reservoir: Towards a Poetic Model of Research in Design. Proceedings of Research into Practice, University of Hertfordshire. https://www.herts.ac.uk/__data/assets/pdf_file/0017/12293/WPIAAD_vol1_rosenberg.pdf (2000)
25. Hannula, M., Suoranta, J., Vaden, T.: Artistic Research. Theories, Methods, Practices. http://www.academia.edu/2396657/Artistic_Research._Theories_Methods_Practices (2005)
26. Thomas, K., Chan, J. (eds.): Handbook of Research on Creativity. Edward Elgar Publishing. http://www.e-elgar.com/shop/handbook-of-research-on-creativity?___website=uk_warehouse (2013)
27. Hockney, D.: Exhibition at the Royal Academy. http://www.theguardian.com/artanddesign/2012/jan/22/david-hockney-bigger-picture-review (2012)
28. Blascovich, J., Bailenson, J.N.: Infinite Reality: Avatars, Eternal Life, New Worlds, and the Dawn of the Virtual Revolution. Harper Collins, William Morrow division (2011)
29. Reinhard, E., Ward, G.S.G.S., Debevec, P., Heidrich, G., Myszkowski, K.: High Dynamic Range Imaging: Acquisition, Display, and Image-Based Lighting, 2nd ed. Morgan Kaufmann (2010)
30. Clark, J.: Netscape Time: The Making of the Billion-Dollar Start-Up That Changed the World. St. Martin's Press, New York (1999)

Chapter 3
Collaboration Methodologies in Art and Design

Abstract Artists such as Leonardo da Vinci were involved with the creation of artistic works and also novel inventions that were intended to serve a purpose in the natural world. Both were seen to be a natural part of the same spirit of enquiry. Collaboration between the arts and the sciences has a long history. In both areas and between them, there are aspects of tension, division, form, and beauty. Art works are traditionally produced in the studio by individual artists. However, computer technology and digital media have increased the variety of tools and environments available to the artist and the designer, and also the potential benefits through sharing and collaboration via telecommunication networks. Visualization and virtual reality bring new dimensions of interactive capability to the artist and the designer in both design and implementation. They also allow art works to be exhibited to global audiences. Digital convergence is bringing the areas of computers, media, and telecommunications closer together, giving rise to new environments and new creative opportunities. Crowd-accelerated developments and creative collaboration via social media are having a transformative effect on the creation, distribution, and the exhibition of creative works, and on traditional art and design processes. Multi-user interaction enables location-based art works to be transformed into new kinds of interactive and dynamic experiences for global viewers. Technology and applications are therefore changing the way ideas are formulated and the way research is developed and advanced. In addition, the ubiquity of new media has facilitated its use to support and develop a number of application domains. The relationship between creativity, collaboration, and artistic works, and their interaction and interplay with social media, brings added dimensions to collaboration.

Keywords Virtual collaboration • creative artworks • digital convergence • creative play • collaboration • Interdisciplinarity • Models of creativity • Innovation in art and design • Social media

3.1 Collaboration Across Traditional Disciplinary Boundaries

If a research area needs tools and facilities from different disciplines, then mechanisms are needed for collaboration. Where there are different traditions and practices in each discipline, these need to be understood by the area benefiting from them.

Computer science is well placed to provide tools and facilities to other disciplines, including art and design. An example, is computer-aided design which has been used for some time because of the advantages it provides. Many of these areas are real-world applications.

Innovation and creativity are complex concepts particularly when applied to new disciplines and new areas of research. From a historical perspective, many exciting innovations have come about because creative people with different perspectives and skills have combined to produce something entirely new. For example it can be argued that the fields of oceanography and cognitive science emerged from multidisciplinary collaborations [1].

Some would argue that as existing disciplines have become well established, then it is more likely that new disciplines will tend to emerge along the boundaries of existing ones, rather than within them, and contain some of the elements from more than one discipline. Thus working at the boundary, or across the boundaries, is likely to be more fruitful in terms of research and developing new knowledge. However, this is not without its risks, as noted by Blackwell et al. [2] because of the silo effect of current disciplines, as well as other factors. It is also well-known that interdisciplinary research tends to be less well understood by reviewers from the established disciplines because it is not regarded as sufficiently pure or traditional, or it may cut across the norms and conventions that have been established within a particular discipline.

A further challenge has been noted by Snow [3] which is the antipathy between the arts and the sciences brought about by a long history of different understandings and modes of discourse about the world, and also the changes brought about by the Scientific Revolution [4]. These different modes of discourse, and understanding of what is regarded as relevant or significant, can make it difficult to accomplish interdisciplinary collaborative research. Yet it may be precisely this research that yields the new insights and the new forms of understanding that open up the future.

The arts and sciences were earlier regarded as operating within different paradigms of understanding making communication across the divide very difficult, if not impossible. However, there are increasing trends towards greater mutual understanding based on a fuller appreciation of the mutual benefits. Disciplinary silos may become increasingly regarded as an historical relic, which are more dependent upon history and context, rather than being able to respond effectively to the opportunities presented by current challenges in the arts, science, and technology.

When interdisciplinary research is carried out in universities, research laboratories, and industry this can also involve working across organisational and resource boundaries. However, they are often working within structures which were set in place to support existing disciplines. Structures and budgets which support the status quo within organised units are generally not flexible enough to support working across different units, unless there are agreed procedures that specifically enable this. This suggests that structures need to be designed to be more open and flexible so that collaboration and innovation can be supported and promoted as a matter of normal practice.

Multi-disciplinary, inter-disciplinary, and trans-disciplinary research are identified by Holzbaur et al. [5] as different aspects of collaboration across boundaries. The existing structures of knowledge and information may be inadequate to cope with their future expansion. Knowledge is increasingly interdisciplinary and the traditional barriers between existing disciplines are being broken down in order to make progress. One way to begin to understand this transition, and start to address this challenge, has been set out by Wilson [6].

Cognitive diversity enables groups to find better solutions and also facilitates finding solutions when the problems are complex. Thus collaboration across discipline boundaries may yield more ground-breaking results than collaboration within a discipline.

One effect of modern technology such as the Internet and the world wide web has been to break down traditional barriers. Formerly, collaborators were co-located within the same physical unit or structure in order to facilitate inter-working. Virtual working now allows researchers to collaborate across time and space, sharing ideas theories, experiments, simulations and results [7, 8]. In theory at least, research and collaboration know no boundaries.

3.2 Ancient Civilisations

In earlier civilisations such as those of China and Greece, the concept of creativity appears to have been absent, at least in the form it is now understood. Art appears to have been seen more as imitation and representation rather than as creation, as the latter was assumed to be the province of the sacred or the divine. The developments of the Renaissance and the Age of Enlightenment brought a more pragmatic view of the world, where created objects served a purpose, whether real or abstract. The development of science and the scientific method progressed by experiment, analysis, and the construction of theories. The latter could be used to test hypotheses and also make predictions. The natural world became both a laboratory and a canvas.

In order to better understand the creative process it is necessary to consider its constituent elements. These include imagination, inspiration, convergence and divergence. The solo artist may develop a variety of approaches depending on the context and the nature of the created work. However, where a number of people are involved in a collaborative creative process, it may be necessary to consider the ways in which talent and expertise can work together in harmony rather than develop

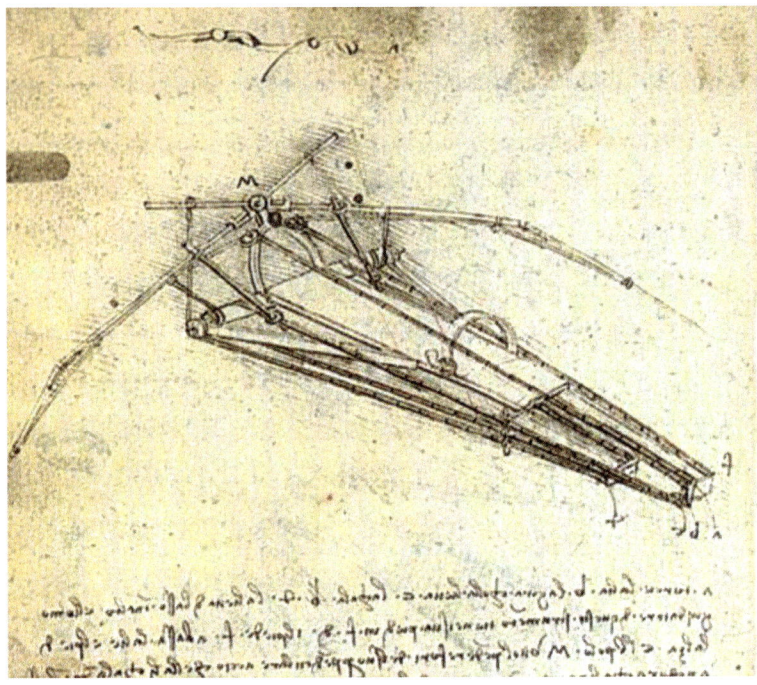

Fig. 3.1 Leonardo da Vinci's design for a flying machine. Public domain – https://commons.wikimedia.org/wiki/File:Design_for_a_Flying_Machine.jpg

a situation of conflict. However, it is possible for creative destruction to generate progress and a positive outcome, and it should not be automatically ruled out. A key aspect to consider for a fruitful collaboration is how best it can be facilitated and developed in order to produce the desired outcome.

It is worth noting that Leonardo da Vinci in the fifteenth century was involved with both the creation of artistic works (e.g. the Mona Lisa) and also novel inventions that served a purpose in the natural world (e.g. Fig. 3.1).

This is an indication that creative genius can transcend the traditional boundaries between disciplines, or work in such a way that the boundaries do not exist. This also suggests that the current boundaries between disciplines may be somewhat arbitrary and based on accumulated past knowledge and traditions rather than current knowledge with its potential for future expansion. However, once disciplinary traditions become established, it can be difficult to establish new ones, especially when they traverse boundaries between the existing disciplines. Incremental advances tend to be preferred because they can be more naturally accommodated within existing disciplines. They are also perceived as less challenging to those who have played a part in establishing the traditions, and therefore have a vested interest in supporting and preserving them.

3.3 Design Education

Interdisciplinary advances also pose a challenge for education curricula, which are based principally on traditional disciplines. In order to address the interdisciplinary challenges, appropriate education and training is required. Yet only slow progress is being made [6]. In addition, Simpson et al. [9] note -

> Evidence suggests that transformational innovation occurs at the intersection of multiple disciplines rather than isolated within them. Design – being both pervasive and inherently interdisciplinary – has the power to transcend many disciplines and help break down the departmental "silos" that hinder such collaborative efforts. Many universities are now struggling to embrace the curricular innovations that are necessary to achieve and sustain interdisciplinary education. [9]

3.4 Art and Science Collaboration

Art Schools are increasingly seeking to encourage collaboration across disciplines in order to further support, and provide evidence for, the concept that art and design is a subject that is at the heart of society. All history may be regarded as the history of ideas. The arts have a responsibility to open up new fields of consciousness and formulate ideas that are able to bring an increased awareness of the history and development of ideas and their value to society. The arts are also able to adopt a more proactive position that inspires as well as informs and communicates. They can provide synergistic connections between arts, science, technology, business and society.

The Angewandte, University of Applied Arts, Vienna, links artistic and scientific disciplines. Its objective is stated as follows –

> The art system in which graduates in "TransArts" will work, oscillates between differing artistic disciplines, theory and practice, concept and artistic techniques, artistic production and its contextualization and communication. Art will not only be taught or learned using traditional teaching forms, but in particular by means of communication, inventiveness and reflective working in an exchange with teachers and students. The "TransArt" study course will attempt to consolidate these processes, which encourage creativity, by means of a new study architecture that will also break through the disciplinary limitations traditional to the universities and thus create a radical, innovative, and in many regards unique, approach to art education. [10]

The Angewandte also facilitates interaction between art and science –

> The objective of the "Art & Science" master degree programme is to investigate the relationships between different artistic and scientific representational cultures and their respective cognitive and research methods. An inter- and transdisciplinary approach and project-oriented education should stimulate interaction between model and theory construction, and the application of methods, in particular, in the arts and sciences. [11]

> This point of view involves the investigation (and the corresponding in-depth study) of social and political processes, the relation, application, and development of artistic and

scientific positions, methods, media, and organisations. Thus, it implies researching an oft-controversial societal thematic space, where the disciplinary, scientific-artistic ivory tower is infiltrated, where students locate and explore – and possibly generate themselves – more or less conspicuous socio-technical ruptures in our society. Prerequisite is a thirst for knowledge that leads to a representation, a creative restructuring of the respective themes, in which the respective application or interweaving of certain artistic or scientific methods or media represents the result and not the departure point of the research. [11]

In the UK, the Wellcome Trust has recognised the importance of synergies between art and science and its Arts Award supports artists to create new work that critically engages audiences with biomedical science. The Wellcome Trust states -

Arts Awards support the creation of new artistic work that critically engages artists and audiences with biomedical science. We strive to work with all art forms and the diverse community we support includes artists, scientists, curators, writers, academics, producers, directors and education officers.

We believe that artists have a distinct approach to understanding and communicating ideas that can illuminate and challenge perceptions within society. We are convinced therefore that the arts have an invaluable role to play in engaging the public with biomedical science.

Arts Awards encourage creative collaborations between art and science. The Wellcome Trust believes that this exchange generates powerful, personal and visceral art and inspires interdisciplinary research and practice that brings benefits to artists and scientists alike. [12]

Therefore artists have a distinctive approach to understanding and communicating ideas that can illuminate and challenge perceptions and understandings within society. This Arts Award has been important in supporting collaborative research between artists and scientists, and encouraging artists to look to scientific research as an inspiration for their work.

Miller [13] and Wilson [14] outline how artists use their skills and expertise to utilise and illuminate the latest discoveries in science. Art and Science Collaborations Inc [15] has the objective of providing information and artists and scientists using science and technology to explore new forms of creative expression and to increase collaboration between these areas.

3.5 Crowd-Accelerated Development

The design and implementation of a creative work is normally done in a studio. When it is complete it may then appear as part of a public exhibition and be available for others to view. Many viewers bring their own preconceptions when they observe an art work which may overlook innovations which lie beneath the surface and, in some cases, were only evident at the design stage.

Anderson [16] observed innovative approaches in the sector and proposed the concept of crowd-accelerated innovation. It presupposes the existence of a community of interest, that they can communicate, and they wish to work together. There may be a multiplicity of motivational factors involved in this participation but the ultimate goal is to benefit the medium of the creative discipline that they are working within. This is represented by the phrase: 'The Crowd, The Light, The Desire'.

This opening up of community access to thinking processes during the development of a concept allows it to be shaped and expanded prior to its final form. The final form of the concept, and any application or deployment of it, should still be regarded as the creation of the initiator. This real-time access to innovative ideas during the conceptual development of a project or art work may be described as an acceleration of the process. It may also generate multiple ideas and multiple pathways to creative outcomes. Thus the creativity processes may be expanded and enhanced.

The way technology mediates these observations and communications is significant. Traditional broadcasting is essentially a one-to-many process. The internet provides a many-to-many process which includes file sharing, blogs, and social media. Although the concept of 'many' initially applies to people, in theory there may be no distinction between organizations, products, processes, events and concepts. Thus the potential for enhancing the creative process is increased on the Internet, and innovation may proceed at a faster pace than with traditional methods of design. The rate of growth of the community of interest is also non-linear, which can generate a greater variety of ideas and inputs. It also allows visual and audio components to be utilised by means of images, videos, or animations.

Thus the sharing of insight and innovation across a group of people has the potential to significantly increase the rate of innovation and also the degree of innovation.

3.6 Visualization and Collaboration

The VISINET project [17, 18] conducted a series of trials of new collaboration methods based on virtual representation and virtual reality techniques over trans-European ATM networks. The objectives of VISINET were to demonstrate the use of advanced 3D visualization systems in the context of shared environments across broadband networks, and investigate the extent to which collaboration using virtual representation reduces deliverable lead times and increases overall user effectiveness. Designers, architects, city planners, and engineers worked collaboratively with virtual 3D models from locations in the Netherlands, Belgium, UK, Ireland, Portugal, and Switzerland. Figure 3.2 shows the network connection diagram.

The initial reaction to VISINET was that it reduced the effect of distance (in geographical terms) and thereby reduced wastage of time. But greater use and familiarity showed that it reduced the *'communication distance'* between parties. VISINET allowed client and supplier to view the physical model from a different perspective, and – by creating more open dialogue – it helped each party to understand the work from the other's point of view.

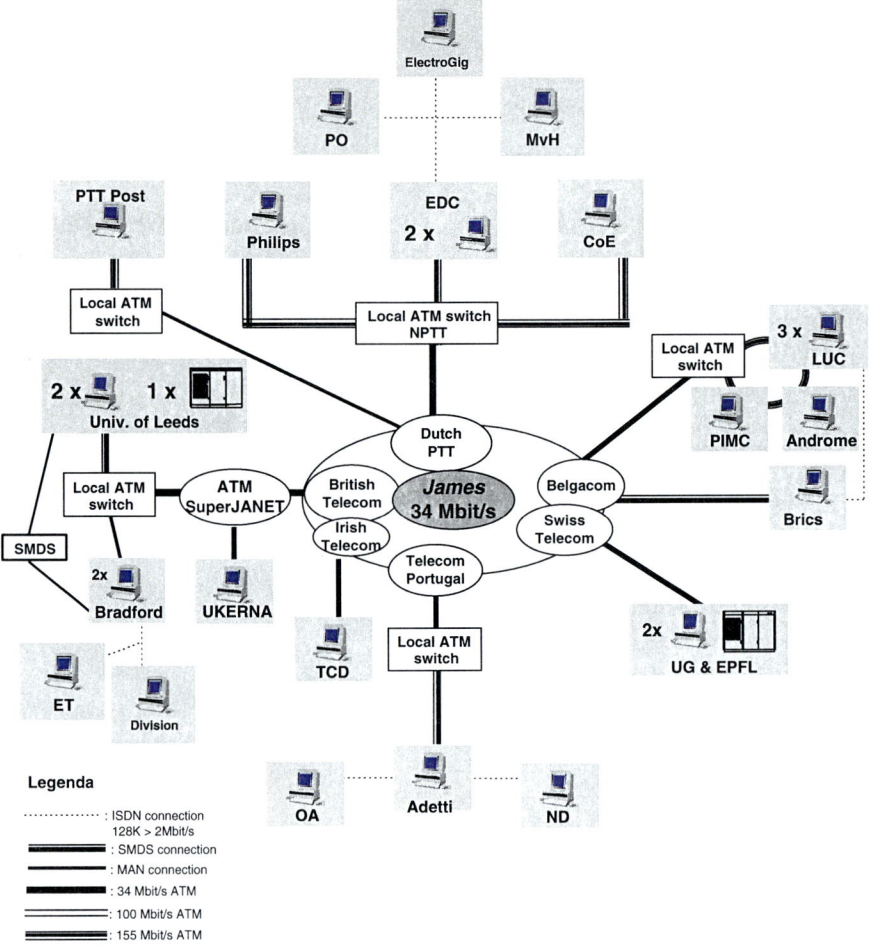

Fig. 3.2 Network connection diagram

The overall belief was that there was a second-stage impact of VISINET which developed out of the initial time saving. This resulted from the combined effect of time saving and greater communication. When these two were combined they gave users the opportunity to increase the quality of the project, so that the end product was better than the original brief. Thus VISINET helped create a *value-added* element which would differentiate it from others. Time savings would mean that the product reached market more quickly, but other methods might also have the same effect. VISINET's added value was in its ability to use time in two dimensions, which both allowed time to be saved and allowed the saved time to be used more effectively.

3.6 Visualization and Collaboration

In the process of doing this, the boundaries between client and supplier diminished, enabling more rapid decision-making. Internal working practices also changed as suppliers became closer to clients, but the true impact was muted, depending on the particular type of company. Where the supplier was design-orientated, the impact was more pronounced because of the higher level of involvement with clients. However, where the internal structure involved engineers or other technicians who would normally take the project on to its next stage of physical manufacture, the impact was restricted.

There is evidence that the use of VISINET did alter working practices and resulted in the re-engineering of business processes. Potential users and many of the actual users came with preconceptions of what new technology might deliver, and this is often expressed in relation to their existing working practices. The key pressures are to save time and money, and therefore the initial reaction to VISINET was measured in these terms.

Actual use of VISINET overcame these difficulties, by allowing users to see how it could enhance not just the communication of the project, but also communication with others working on the project. Thus time savings are re-invested into the project, allowing the production of a better value-added product, and the development of a better relationship with others, which furthers business development (even at a distance).

In summary, the potential benefits consolidated into several major areas:

- Reduction in overall operating costs
- Improvement of overall product and process quality
- Reduction of time to market
- Savings on time and travel
- Opening up new commercial opportunities
- Improvement of decision making
- Reengineering of the organization and its working practices

A European project on Multimedia Assets for Industrial Design (MAID) [19] with 15 partners was designed to demonstrate the viability of multimedia and virtual reality telematics as an economically justified and professionally effective tool for the design industry. As a telematics project using ISDN and ATM, it was expected to have a significant impact on the professional market for high-speed multimedia communications, and to extend knowledge and awareness of the technologies' capacities both inside and outside the professional community. MAID developed and demonstrated systems which allowed designers and industry to -

- interactively access multimedia databases
- integrate data into their own design computing environment
- participate in distant work groups and receive on-line design tools and services
- implement projects at a distance

The MAID project designed, tested and demonstrated a range of high-level Information Services for the industrial design sector, aimed at improving the competitiveness of the design-based industries and professions. It addressed a wide range of information engineering problems and demonstrated effective systems of multimedia data exchange. It offers scalable solutions for asset trading involving existing technologies. The information engineering research covered tasks in the key areas of the creation of multimedia assets; the creation of a networked information centre managing the dissemination of data; methods of connecting different users' environments, incorporating disparate data, and connecting the service to the design and prototyping chain; data finding, selection, tracking and payment. The development of novel and user-friendly interface models was a particularly important element of the project. MAID demonstrated networked services based on the concepts of a Design Information Centre and a Design Services Centre for test by target users as a prelude to commercial exploitation. The system handled 'conventional' multimedia data assets (including video), 3D CAD data and simulation data, and allow the integration of VR design tools. It was conceived as a transaction-based system with a commercial charging mechanism. The business plan also included the exploitation of generic sub-products and information engineering solutions developed in the project.

3.7 Contemporary Collaborations

Catmull [20] describes how to achieve an optimum coalescence of art, innovation and business arising out the experience of creating a series of award-winning animated films. Receiving 27 Academic Awards to date, these films stand as a testimony to the creative processes involved and what can be achieved with a combination of storytelling, plot, emotional authenticity, believable characters, and state of the art animation techniques.

Hegarty [21] presents the view that everyone can be creative. It is more a matter of individual context and approach rather than compliance with existing rules. Shiu [22] notes the interdisciplinary nature of creativity research. In addition, creative and interdisciplinary thinkers have abilities that are being increasingly recognised and valued in a range of activities including business, research, and the media. Their ideas and ways of working are increasingly being imported into businesses to challenge existing ways of thinking and working. Many companies are actively seeking creative methods of change management in order to unlock latent potential, harness abilities to think outside current norms, and increase competitiveness.

Rush [23] summarises how contemporary artists use technology in their work and how new technologies have enabled new ways of collaborating to be developed.

> *The final avant-garde, if one should call it that, of the twentieth century is that art which engages the most enduring revolution in a century of revolutions: the technological revolution. Initiated by inventions outside the world of art, technology-based art (encompassing and range of practices from photography to film to video to virtual reality, and much else in between) has directed art into areas once dominated by engineers and technicians.*

3.7 Contemporary Collaborations

Fine art practice has also been able to exploit technology and new media and challenged the traditional hierarchies of painting and sculpture. This has produced new paradigms of creativity and practice. Heald and Liggett [24, 25] have explored the relationship between traditional and new media and collaborative opportunities. This has challenged theories and methodologies within fine art practice and has created new concepts and artworks. This collaborative practice has stimulated new discourses, with new kinds of interactions that have resulted in creative advances.

Painting and filmmaking provided the starting points for the creative collaborations. The work brings together narrative, sensory intelligence, and kinaesthetic learning. It has developed from the videos and writings of Viola [26]. Filmmaking involves both writing and recording. Its processes can involve writing a script, turning on a camera, and recording a scene – sometimes in unprepared environments. In this sense, it is venturing into the unknown. Enactments of the work could take place in performance spaces, such as in Art Galleries or Dance Theatres. However, they could also take place in non-conventional spaces, such as on public transport, in the home, or in hospitals. Thus they were able to transcend traditional boundaries and merge art and real life situations.

Photographs were also used as the basis for a process of painting. A photograph is a snap-shot in time, and it captures a scene at a particular moment. The painting process sought to give new life and energy to the photograph, to enable its constituent parts to be emotionally processed. The work explores the concept of *psychological resonance,* which is the metaphoric vibration resulting from an inner dialogue between 'subject' and 'object'. Thus there are stages in the creative process where the destination of the process cannot be fully articulated. However, the processes of interacting with the particular medium using its constituent tools (e.g. pen, paintbrush, camera, or computer) can involve an element of serendipitous play, where the outcome is not known in advance (the interim states being defined as *in-between-ness*). This may be regarded as different to traditional approaches to an art work where a scene is known in full outline from the beginning, and the artist progressively fills in more detail in a systematic and incremental way to bring the outline to life.

A number of organisations have collaborated with the artists including schools, public organisations, private businesses and public services. This has provided an interchange of contexts and experiences which has broadened the research aspects of the work and stimulated new dimensions of thinking and creating. Such shared experiences have enabled collaborations to develop in a non-hierarchical way with the creative outputs such as painting and film artworks being mutually shared. Examples of such pieces of artwork are *Fragmentary Chronicles II (2012)* (Fig. 3.3) and *Poesy II* (2012) (Fig. 3.4). This synergistic combination of media, tools, and creativity has opened up new possibilities for the future, as well as bridging the gap between the artist and the public. The latter have become full partners in the creative process.

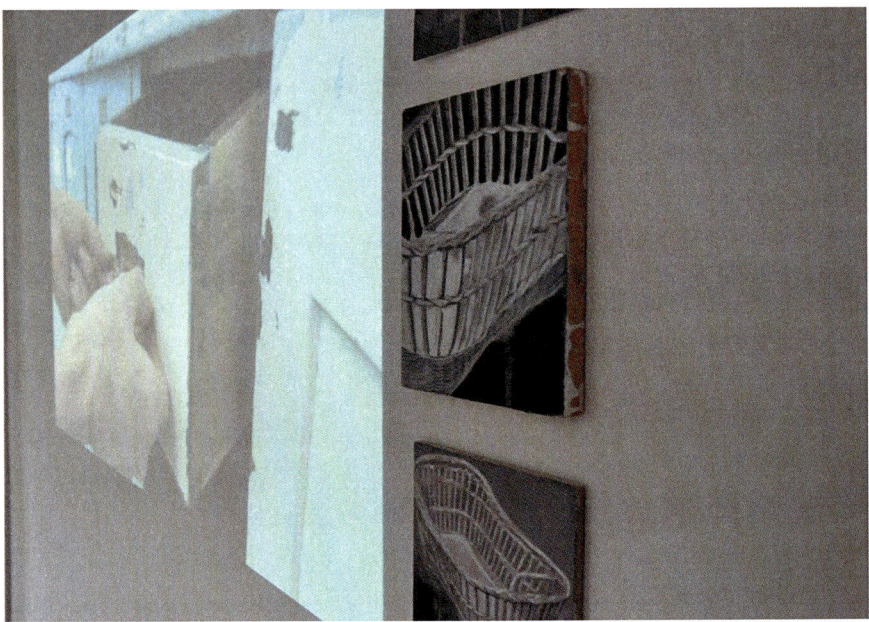

Fig. 3.3 Fragmentary Chronicles II (Bird-Jones & Heald, Heald & Liggett, 2012) (Reproduced by permission)

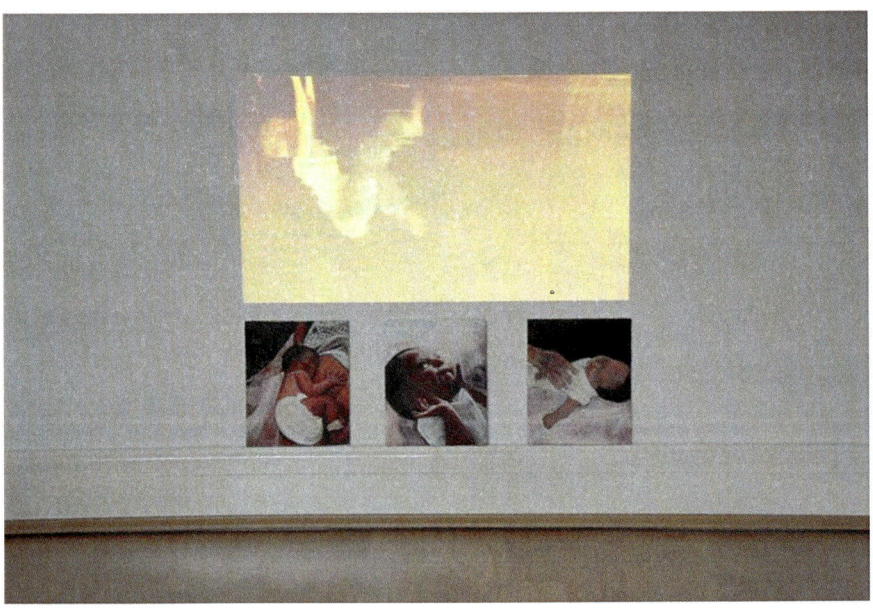

Fig. 3.4 Poesy II (Heald & Farris, Heald & Liggett, 2012) (Reproduced by permission)

3.8 Conclusions

Fig. 3.5 White (Heald & Liggett, 2009) (Reproduced by permission)

These collaborations have expanded through a variety of media including video, installation, and photography. It has thus become a visual language which brings together different aspects of painting and film. The work engages with a variety of diverse practitioners such as artists, scientists, medical doctors, and a number of other academics [27].

The artworks have also been exhibited via live web-streaming to remote audiences, and video links enabled live participation in the performance. Engaging in 'play' has been observed to have a therapeutic effect. According to Winnicott [27], 'play' relates to an individual's capacity to live creatively.

These creative processes are developing an intuitive way to think through the lens. An example is the film *White* (2009) (Fig. 3.5).

3.8 Conclusions

The boundary between technology and society is becoming increasingly blurred due to the ubiquity of computing technology and the ways in which it can be integrated into the everyday environment in a seamless way. For example, the modern car may have at least 30 microprocessor controlled devices and luxury cars up to 100. These perform more or less automatic operations and assist in the operation of the vehicle. Thus computers may be embedded, or they can be operated by the user as a tool. Both these forms can be utilised by art and design.

The boundary between the real and the virtual is blurring. Design projects operating over telecommunication networks have demonstrated the power of bringing together physically distant groups of designers into a shared virtual space where design actions and iterations can be visualized and discussed in real-time. The effect of design changes on the end-to-end design to manufacture process can also be simulated, determined and evaluated. This environment also allows virtual exhibitions, galleries and museums to reach global audiences as well as local ones. Interaction allows the sharing of different experiences, cultures and backgrounds.

The boundary between the technical and the social is blurring. The many-to-many communication environment supported by the Internet and social media allows a greater degree of involvement and sharing by the community. Social media opens up new dimensions of interaction and participation.

By utilising technology, artists are now able to reach out to new communities. Thus, they contribute to an evolving arts and cultural economy. They can also provide new ways to support a variety of interdisciplinary applications for which art and design can provide added value.

Collaboration enables new kinds of environments to be developed and supported. In turn these enable the generation of new creative processes which are able to transcend tradition and history. The artist is able to regard technology as an assistant which is able to facilitate new dimensions of thinking and new directions of creativity and discovery.

Further Reading

Beard, M., Henderson, J.: Classical Art: From Greece to Rome. Oxford University Press, p. 304 (2001)
Cairo, A.: The Functional Art: An Introduction to Information Graphics and Visualization. New Riders, p. 384 (2012)
Clunas, C.: Art in China. Oxford University Press, p. 288 (2009)
Lowgren, J., Reimer, B.: Collaborative Media: Production, Consumption, and Design Interventions. MIT Press, p. 208 (2013)
Paldam, C.S., Wamberg, J.: Art, Technology and Nature. Ashgate, p. 276 (2015)
Vasari, G.: Leonardo da Vinci. Penguin Classics, p. 64 (2015)
White, M.: Leonardo da Vinci: The First Scientist. Abacus, p. 384 (2001)

References

1. Cummings, J. N., Kiesler, S.: Collaborative Research Across Disciplinary and Organizational Boundaries. Carnegie Mellon University, HCI Institute. http://repository.cmu.edu/hcii/93/ (2005)
2. Blackwell, A., Wilson, L., Boulton, C., Knell, J.: Creating Value Across Boundaries: Maximising the Return for Interdisciplinary Innovation. NESTA Research Report, May 2010 http://www.nesta.org.uk/library/documents/creating_value_across_boundaries_may10.pdf (2010)
3. Snow, C.P.: The Two Cultures. Cambridge University Press (1959) ISBN 0-521-45730-0

References

4. Principe, L.M.: The Scientific Revolution: A Very Short Introduction. Oxford University Press, Oxford (2011)
5. Holzbaur, U.D., Lategan, L.O.K., Dyason, K., Kokt, D.: Seven Imperatives for Research. SunMedia Bloemfontein (2012) ISBN 978-1-920382-13-1
6. Wilson, A.G.: Knowledge Power: Interdisciplinary Education for a Complex World. Routledge, Abingdon (2012)
7. Reeve, C.M.: Presence in virtual theater presence. MIT Press **9**(2), 209–213 (2000). doi:10.1162/105474600566727
8. Joslin, C., Molet, T., Magnenat-Thalmann, N., Esmerado, J., Thalmann, D., Palmer, I.J., Chilton, N., Earnshaw, R.A.: Sharing attractions on the net with VPARK. IEEE Comput. Graph. Appl. **21**(1), 61–71 (2001). ISSN 0272-1716. http://www.computer.org/portal/web/csdl/doi/10.1109/38.895134
9. Simpson, T.W., Parkinson, M., Celento, D., Chen, W., McKenna, A., Colgate, E., Norman, D., Papalambros, P., Gonzalez, R., Roth, B., Leifer, L.: Navigating the barriers to interdisciplinary design education: lessons learned from the NSF Design Workshop Series. Proceedings of the ASME Design Engineering Technical Conference. **6**:627–637 (2010)
10. Angewandte TransArts. http://www.dieangewandte.at/jart/prj3/angewandte/main.jart?rel=en&content-id=1292155820051&reserve-mode=active
11. Art and Science. http://www.dieangewandte.at/jart/prj3/angewandte/main.jart?rel=en&content-id=1292155820052&reserve-mode=active
12. Wellcome Trust Arts Awards. http://www.wellcome.ac.uk/funding/public-engagement/funding-schemes/arts-awards/
13. Miller, A.I.: Colliding Worlds: How Cutting-Edge Science is Redefining Contemporary Art. W. W. Norton and Company, New York (2014)
14. Wilson, S.: Art + Science Now: How Scientific Research and Technological Innovation Are Becoming Key to 21st Century Aesthetics. Thames & Hudson, London (2012)
15. Art and Science Collaborations Inc. http://www.asci.org/
16. Anderson, C., Curato, T., Anderson, C.: Crowd accelerated innovation. Wired. Available at: http://www.wired.com/2010/12/ff_tedvideos/ (2010)
17. Lamotte, W., Earnshaw, R.A., Van Reeth, F., Flerackers, E., Mena de Matos, E.: VISINET: collaborative 3D visualization and virtual reality over trans-European ATM networks. IEEE Comp. Graph. Appl. Spec. Issue 3D Multimed. Inf. Superhighway IEEE Comp. Soc. **17**(2), 66–75 (1997)
18. 3D Visualization over Networks (VISINET). http://cordis.europa.eu/infowin/acts/analysys/concertation/chains/si/home/ch_sid/visinetoutput.html
19. Multimedia Assets for Industrial Design (MAID). http://cordis.europa.eu/project/rcn/34040_en.html
20. Catmull, E.: Creativity, Inc.: Overcoming the Unseen Forces That Stand in the Way of True Inspiration. Bantam Press, p. 368 (2014)
21. Hegarty, J.: Hegarty on Creativity: There Are No Rules. Thames and Hudson, London, p. 128 (2014)
22. Shiu, E. (Ed): Creativity Research: An Inter-Disciplinary and Multi-Disciplinary Research Handbook. Routledge, London, p. 356 (2014)
23. Rush, M.: New Media in Late 20th Century Art. Thames and Hudson, London (1999)
24. Earnshaw, R.A., Liggett, S., Heald, K.: Interdisciplinary Collaboration Methodologies in Art, Design and Media. Proceedings of International Conference on Internet Technologies and Applications. pp. 381–388, ISBN 978-0-946881-81-9, UK (2013) Download PDF
25. Liggett, S., Heald, K., Earnshaw, R.A., Thompson, E., Excell, P.S.: Collaborative Research in Art, Design and New Media – Challenges and Opportunities. Proceedings of Internet Technologies and Applications. For more information see: http://ita15.net/ita-art-expo/DownloadPDF (2015)

26. Viola, B.: Reasons for Knocking at an Empty House: Writings 1973–1994. Thames and Hudson, London (1995)
27. Heald, K.: 'Dream Films' and Research as Collaborative Practice in Arts & Science Methodologies. PhD Thesis, Leeds Metropolitan University (2014)
28. Winnicott, D.W.: Playing and Reality. Routledge, London (1971)

Chapter 4
Creativity and Creative Processes in Art and Design

Abstract Humans have created since the dawn of civilisation. Generating a design, leaving a mark, producing an artefact, communicating a concept, or changing a tradition, all involve the transformation of an idea into reality. This expression is often an advance on the status quo and contributes something new. At the same time such creations, and the ideas behind them, are inescapably connected to the social and cultural experiences of individuals and communities within which they were created. They also often play a significant part in the development of cultures, traditions, and the economic growth of organisations and nations. They often define these cultures, secure their place in history, and provide a legacy for future generations. An important component of creativity is communication. This presupposes a degree of openness on the part of the communicator and the recipients(s). Such openness indicates a readiness to receive new ideas and new cultural contexts, and also reciprocate by sharing information and searching for new explanations of disparate concepts. Thus the development of human creativity has depended to a large extent on speech, writing, images, reading, observing, and printing. The latter took a major step forward with the development of the printing press. This has greatly facilitated the process of learning and the sharing of information. Increased potential for communication has led to communities being more open and innovative. Multiple channels are now available. Open ways of thinking and working are able to support the generation of new concepts and ideas more readily than closed environments. In addition, the increase in the use of digital environments provides new frameworks, tools, and opportunities for the expression of new ideas and new designs, as well as providing new kinds of interactions and environments within which ideas can be generated, displayed, and explored. The extent to which new technologies may advance the creativity process is discussed. Factors governing creativity and the degree to which they may be augmented and enhanced are analysed. The massive increase in the volume of information being generated and circulated by digital systems is analogous to that brought about by the printing press, and could thus constitute a new technological paradigm. The extent to which this may constitute a paradigm shift on the status quo is analysed. Extracting meaning and knowledge from very large sets of information is a significant challenge often requiring multidisciplinary expertise of the kind provided by teams of mathematicians, statisticians, social scientists, data visualization specialists, and presentation experts.

Keywords Creative processes • Digital environments • Virtual design • Virtual exhibition • Cyberworlds • Social media interactions • Creative industries • Paradigm shift

4.1 Defining Creativity

Creativity is characterised by the generation of new ideas that are able to transform the original situation into a different one. Such developments may be iterative advancements on the status quo or they may be completely new. In both cases they open up new possibilities and new horizons. The development may be a new idea, a new principle, or a new way of looking at an existing situation, or it may be a new system, or a new physical object such as a book, sculpture, or painting. In the latter areas, it is clear that creativity can play a key role in the generation of new products and services that have value to those who wish to use them. The value may be in terms of artistic or aesthetic form, or in efficacy and efficiency, and possibly also functionality and performance.

The age of the Renaissance opened up new ways of thinking and creating, partly by a rediscovery of elements of Greek philosophy and partly by its expression in art, architecture, literature and science. In particular, the development of perspective in painting – the approximation on a two-dimensional surface of an image as seen by the eye Later, the Industrial Revolution was able to take new discoveries in mathematics, physics, chemistry, biology, and engineering, and transform them into new products and services for science, technology, and society. It is useful in retrospect to consider what misunderstandings and obstacles had to be overcome, and what gaps in knowledge and understanding had to be bridged, in order to provide the opportunities for new ways forward to be developed. In other words, what are the preconditions for creativity to operate? Does it depend on the innate capability of the human mind to provide these bridges and leaps of understanding, or does it depend on the external elements in the world being at a particular point of development so that the next steps can then be conceived and realised? Or is it a mixture of the two elements – which may vary in different times and circumstances, and across disciplines?

An important component of creativity is communication. This presupposes a degree of openness on the part of the communicator and the recipients(s). Such openness indicates a readiness to receive new ideas and new cultural contexts, and also reciprocate by sharing information. Thus the development of human creativity has depended to a large extent on speech, writing, images, reading, observing, and printing. The latter took a major step forward with the development of the printing press. This has greatly facilitated the process of learning and the sharing of information.

4.2 Historical Examples of Creativity

Tools and materials have been used from the earliest days of cave paintings more than 35,000 years ago to express views of the world and conceptions of reality. They were early forms of communication and creativity.

4.3 Interaction and Creativity

It is not known what purpose such cave paintings served, though various theories have been advanced. However, one aspect of their production is clear. They all involve an interaction of a human with some kind of tool or writing device, and also some pigments where colour is involved, or a direct interaction (e.g. by a hand) with the external environment. The human has used the tool and pigments to create a painting on the wall of a cave to represent in visual form some aspect of their society and its relationship to the animal kingdom (where animals are pictured in the painting). Thus the human is not just depicting their relationship to the animal in some way, but is also interacting with tools and the cave in order to represent this. The relationship to the human (e.g. as a hunter) could have been preserved in some form of verbal tradition, or a practice handed down from one generation to the next through the experience of hunting animals. But the key point here is that something *additional* to this was also practiced and has been preserved. It is also evidence of communication and the sharing of information. Whatever purpose it served at the time, it is a form of creative expression that arose out of their experiences with the external world. In other words, key aspects of the creative process are the interaction with the environment to generate it and the new output that is produced and preserved. A human's ability to interact with their environment in a conscious and creative way is what distinguishes them from the animals, although there are numerous examples of animals using creative tools. The latter interact with the environment, but more by instinct and habit than by conscious reasoning with a view to further development and planning. Humans used tools from the earliest eras, formed from various kinds of stones (Fig. 4.1) and ground into shapes.

Stonehenge in the UK is an example of an early stone construction dating back to around 3,000 BC (Fig. 4.2). It is believed to be some form of burial ground. Certain stones within the configuration line up with the sunset of the winter solstice and sunrise of the solstice. As there are no written records from this period it is not known for certain what its purpose was, though from the remains that have been found, it appears to have been in use for at least 500 years.

The use of tools and natural materials therefore resulted in a construction which has preserved the past. They must have performed measurements in order to decide

Fig. 4.1 An array of Neolithic artifacts, including bracelets, axe heads, chisels, and polishing tools. Courtesy of "Néolithique 0001". Licensed under CC BY-SA 2.5 via Commons – https://commons.wikimedia.org/wiki/File:N%C3%A9olithique_0001.jpg#/media/File:N%C3%A9olithique_0001.jpg

Fig. 4.2 Stonehenge "Stonehenge, Condado de Wiltshire, Inglaterra, 2014-08-12, DD 09" by Diego Delso. Licensed under CC BY-SA 4.0 via Commons – https://commons.wikimedia.org/wiki/File:Stonehenge,_Condado_de_Wiltshire,_Inglaterra,_2014-08-12,_DD_09.JPG#/media/File:Stonehenge,_Condado_de_Wiltshire,_Inglaterra,_2014-08-12,_DD_09.JPG

where to place the stones. They must also have used some kind of tools to move them to the site and place them in an upright position. Interaction of humans with the environment was therefore key to its production.

The human's potential for creativity therefore has been augmented by various aspects of the environment.

4.4 Digital Environments and Creativity

Interaction in digital environments often supplies the user with tools (interaction devices) and a visual representation of the object as it is designed or manipulated. In some cases the visual representation can be a walk-in environment (such as a Cave – Fig. 4.3) where the user is surrounded by a virtual representation as if it were the real world (as in an aircraft flight simulator). Thus the human's potential for creativity can be facilitated by technology, or if the technology is not fully oriented to the user's way of working then it can act as an inhibitor and a constraint.

The name is thought to be a reference to the allegory of the Cave in Plato's *Republic* in which a philosopher contemplates perception, reality and illusion – though this Cave was a constrained environment compared to the real world. The user's immersion in the Cave as depicted in Fig. 4.3 is thought to provide an additional sense of realism over and above that which would be experienced by observing a 2D image or even a 3D stereoscopic image with depth cues. It has also been suggested that immersion of a human in an environment of this kind provokes a kind of "suspension of disbelief" – so that even though the world displayed is artificial, it is made to feel more real because the observer feels they are a participant

Fig. 4.3 A Cave "CAVE Crayoland" by User:Davepape – own work (self-photograph using timer). Licensed under Public Domain via Commons – https://commons.wikimedia.org/wiki/File:CAVE_Crayoland.jpg#/media/File:CAVE_Crayoland.jpg

within it. Virtual environments have been successfully used for the presentation and simulation of objects and spaces. Do they offer any advantages in the design process? Research studies in architectural design in immersive virtual environments have demonstrated that designers perceive and understand volumes, spaces, and spatial relationships better than in 2D environments [1]. Virtual environments also assist in the exploration of 3D spaces.

Computer technology offers the user the ability to extrapolate from the current situation and project into the future. Millions of permutations can be calculated in a fraction of a second. Clearly these cannot all be explored on a human time scale, but appropriate selection of the ones likely to be the most interesting can be performed by interactive analysis assisted by artificial intelligence techniques. Of course, seeking to define what 'is likely to be the most interesting' will involve some rules and procedures that can be expressed in computer form. In the first instance therefore, this will require human input to select which aspects of a class of creative works are regarded as the most interesting, and also how this might change in the future. This process may be initially deterministic but may subsequently on execution become indeterminate. Such a process may therefore generate something new, original, and unexpected.

A European project, VPARK, extended collaborative virtual environments (such as VISINET, Chap. 3) to include virtual humans to represent a Virtual Entertainment Park [2, 3]. Two demonstrators were trialled – virtual theatre rehearsal and virtual orchestra rehearsal. These enabled geographically separated participants to come together in the virtual environment in real-time and perform the kind of scenarios they would normally do when co-located in a physical rehearsal. The objective was to determine which aspects of the rehearsal process could be successfully accomplished in virtual environments and which could not. Virtual rehearsal was found to be particularly successful for those stages of the rehearsal which involved script reading and the path planning of the actors on the virtual stage. The actors could then come together on the physical stage for the final phase of rehearsals. The script was fully rehearsed and the movements of all the actors had been planned and rehearsed. Thus substantial savings in travel time and cost were accomplished. The virtual orchestra rehearsal project was less successful because it transpired that the players in the orchestra often rely on very rapid visual interaction with the conductor with regard to timing and emphasis, which is not easy to replicate in virtual environments due to the latency in the network links. It is difficult to assess how effective these environments were in increasing creative opportunities, but they certainly speeded up the more routine tasks.

A European project, VISTA, had the objective of creating interactive broadcast drama [4, 5]. It implemented a generic and extensible telematics platform that supported the execution of scenarios in the domain of interactive television, which could be regarded as the realization of a virtual studio. The networked platform enabled the generation of innovative interactive teleservices for homes. These took the form of television programmes broadcast over conventional television channels, with the important difference that viewers at home were able to direct, and to interact with, the programme being viewed. The image content of the programme was generated (and transmitted) in real-time by high-end graphics computers and networks. As the viewers at home needed a cost-effective way of interacting with the programmes, the existing and affordable infrastructure of the traditional telephone networks was utilized for feeding the viewers' interaction back to the programme being transmitted which was controlled by servers. The number of simultaneous viewers that actively could participate in the interaction depended upon the programme (i.e. the application) at issue, and varied from just a few to several hundreds.

The VISTA project developed and tested the following four specific applications on the platform:

- **Interactive Drama**: Creation of an interactive television program (simultaneously on three channels) in which viewers participated in a cultural drama.
- **Language Teaching**: Creation of an interactive series in which viewers learned foreign languages by interacting with virtual language teachers.
- **Defensive Driving**: Creation of an interactive television program which learned the traffic rules by means of driving through a virtual environment.
- **Interactive Presenter**: Creation of a virtual presenter that could be controlled remotely.

These applications could be considered as being supported within a virtual studio environment which was capable of being interacted with, and changed by, remote users.

The production of creative works with the assistance of computers and virtual environments has prompted a more detailed reflection on the processes of human creativity. Computer-assisted learning prompted a more detailed consideration of pedagogy and human learning processes, and models of artificial intelligence prompted a more detailed examination of human intelligence. Providing a degree of externalisation of human processes has enabled them to be examined more objectively than formerly, though this is still a matter of some debate [6–9].

The increasing ubiquity of the digital environment has therefore opened up new possibilities for iterating through a variety of ideas and different visual representations at a greater rate than was possible using previous manual methods. It is debatable whether this enhances creativity per se, but it certainly provides a greater variety of options for the artist or designer to choose from. In addition, when data is held in digital form it is possible to run simulations and have virtual 'walk-throughs'. The latter is particularly important in the area of architectural design and also the design of 3D objects such as sculptures. A virtual walk-through of a building design can provide an experience close to that of reality and enable a human to experience first-hand how the building would appear when it is constructed. In this way, any deficiencies or short-comings in how the building is experienced, or how it sits in relationship to its environment, can be addressed before the design is finalised and implemented. With digital designs it is also possible to optimise the designs for situations where there are internal or external constraints, for example, in the total budget for the materials for a building, or construction costs, or in the implementation of an art work. It can also take into account situations where it is desirable that eco-factors be addressed – either in the materials used, or their effect upon the environment in which they are to be installed. The cumulative effect of the digital environment is therefore able to provide the artist and designer with a comprehensive framework of facilities. These include tools for design, mock-ups, real-time simulations, analysis of final representations, and usability testing of final configurations of objects, architectural spaces, and the environments which contain them. Although physical 3D scale models gave previous generations of builders a good understand of the structure of the building and how it would sit in its environment, it was difficult to fully understand how it would feel at full scale, particularly to a person moving from room to room inside the building.

The history of computing has demonstrated that its initial potential was not recognised –

> *What shall we do to get rid of Babbage and his calculating machine? Surely if completed it would be worthless as far as science is concerned?* (Sir Robert Peel, Prime Minister of Great Britain in 1842 [10]).

Therefore today it may be difficult to fully envisage how far computers and associated technology will continue to transform the way information is processed and the way we think about creating in the future.

4.5 Enhancing Creativity

An art exhibition is a place where audiences meet works of art that are themselves a form of exposition. In the past, such exhibitions have been static and for a particular time period and therefore had to be viewed by visitors within that time frame. They have also been mainly works of art such as pictures and drawings, sculptures, or installation art which contained various object components.

For groups of people who have common interests, but no opportunity to meet due to geographical separation, online collaboration can provide new opportunities and new environments for sharing and creating.

Art galleries are able to move from static displays fixed in time and space to more flexible virtual environments capable of attracting visitors on a global basis. In addition, it provides the context for the development of collaborative art works and interactive exhibits.

Liggett et al. [11] and Earnshaw et al. [12] detail projects which bring together artists, scientists, and social media in collaborative processes. It has been demonstrated that these collaborations deliver added value to all participants and enable research and development to proceed at a faster pace. This subject is examined in more detail in the chapter on collaboration.

Enhancing creativity may be accomplished by -

- Increasing the diversity of the participants
- Providing anonymity
- Providing creativity triggers through illustrations of tangible products -

- Prototype
- Simulation
- Storyboards
- Mockups
- Graphical presentations

Carroll [13] explores whether and how creativity and rationale can have mutually facilitative interactions. Designs usually serve a particular purpose and conform to certain expectations and norms. Designs often open up new issues, raise new questions, and produce new understandings of aesthetics. However, this can also create tension in contexts where creativity produces a significant departure from the status quo, and where the effect on those who observe the design may be unpredictable.

Defining the process of analysis to enable it to be done automatically by a computer requires the definition of the key parameters. The use of artificial intelligence techniques may provide a degree of augmentation of human capability and present new options and possibilities not conceived of initially by the human mind. This raises the question of in what sense could a machine be described as having creativity? In what sense would this relate to human creativity? If one of the objectives of Google's acquisition of DeepMind in 2014 was to improve the capability of machines to be able to think more like humans, then it will be interesting to see how far computers are able to produce creative solutions to current challenges and problems in order to go beyond what humans are currently able to do [14]. Clearly one of the advantages is direct access to the world's information in Google's databases in forms other than searching for a match to a query. Knowing the right question to ask is often a large part of the problem space. If the question is not known in advance, can new applications of Google's databases provide new and innovative ideas derived from the current information that has been collected and stored? The issue of whether machines could surpass the capabilities of humans is an ongoing debate [15].

4.6 New Media in Cyberworlds

With the rise of new media and digital art forms there has been increasing scope for a wider variety of art objects, particular those that are able to interact with audiences. Such interactions may change the art work, or the perspective of the viewer, or both. In addition, time-based media such as video may be used in exhibitions either in free-standing mode, or be able to receive input from viewers to change the content of the video being displayed. This raises the concept of exhibitions which both change over time resulting from interactions with audiences, and which may no longer be constrained to a particular fixed time period. In particular, a virtual exhibition can be open to global audiences which can result in a sharing of cultural and ethical experiences across national and international boundaries. This introduces the concept of exhibition spaces that are borderless with respect to time, space, and audiences [16, 17]. An artist who wishes to exhibit their work in this rapidly changing environment faces two principal challenges. The first is to demonstrate the relevance of the art to today's audiences and the rapidly changing environment. The second is to articulate forms of art which are capable of transcending the boundaries of past traditions and demonstrate new horizons and new opportunities. The Art Expo at Wrexham Glyndwr University in association with an international conference is an example of what can be accomplished in these new environments [18, 19], i.e. the exhibition has both a physical and virtual presence.

4.7 Interaction and Collaboration

Interactive technology and social media are also changing the way research and development is advanced and companies do business. Increased potential for communication has led to communities being more open and innovative. Multiple channels are now available.

The potential for more creative solutions to challenging problems is increasingly being recognised. It enables collaborative working in areas of mutual interest. Devices and interfaces to applications are becoming increasingly mobile and intelligent. From anywhere to anywhere is now the nature of business. A business can have both local and global reach. Use of the cloud and social media by business and commerce is increasing. These online resources will affect and drive the future [20]. Many businesses are moving from operating only at a macro level to also operating at a micro level as they are able to capitalise on the expanding domain of globally aggregated micro-information from the market place.

4.8 Crowd Accelerated Innovation

The Internet is now ubiquitous and increasingly integrated into everyday activities such as work and leisure. Clark [21] argues that one Internet year is equivalent to seven calendar years, and therefore the more significant the Internet became, the faster the processes and developments would take place. The Deloitte Mobile Consumer Survey 2015 [22] has identified that 76 % of the UK population now own a smartphone and collectively look at their smartphones over a billion times a day. Thus 76 % of the UK population are effectively carrying the Internet with them and connectivity is ubiquitous. The increase in the number of potential collaborators is therefore not just physical but also becomes virtual through the Internet and online social media [23]. This facilitates crowd-accelerated developments [24]. This can also have unexpected and serendipitous effects when new collaborators join in from different cultures and with different backgrounds. They bring their own unique and diverse contributions that can be transformative in their effect on the status quo. Thus the Internet and online collaborations not only bring accelerated developments, they also bring new kinds of environments and interactions which are ubiquitous and pervasive, and which can have creative outcomes that were not initially planned or expected. A significant quantum effect in creativity and collaboration can take place, simply because of the large volume of potential collaborators [25, 26] and also communities [27–29]. Internet time breaks down the traditional barriers of geography and distance.

Research frontiers of human computer interaction include the desire that interaction be more centered around human needs and capabilities, and that the human environment be considered in virtual environments and in other contextual information processing activities. The overall goal is to make users more effective in their information or communication tasks by reducing learning times, speeding performance, lowering error rates, facilitating retention and increasing subjective satisfaction. Improved designs can dramatically increase effectiveness for users who range from novices to experts and who are in diverse cultures with varying educational backgrounds. It also provides significant opportunities for Small and Medium Enterprises (SMEs), freelancers, and independent artists to more easily collaborate with others in areas of joint interest. This has proved particularly useful in the development of the creative industries.

4.9 Can Creativity Be Developed?

Creativity is both intrinsic and capable of development. It is known that the way children explore their environment from an early age contributes substantially to their learning and development. Processes which encourage exploration and experimentation are likely to lead to new outcomes. These processes are based on the use of imagination, the testing of the current environment, and the ability to aggregate the information that is assimilated. This implies that creativity can be stimulated and enhanced. Increased communication and openness contribute to this.

Asimov [30] observed that creative advances were made when people were open to new information, made connections between entities that formerly were regarded as disparate, and were motivated to search for new explanations.

4.10 Can Creativity Be Measured?

How can the difference between a new idea and an old one be evaluated? Various measures have been considered such as originality, utility, aesthetic value, and potential commercial success. Guildford [31] pioneered the study of creativity using psychometrics and conducted numerous tests designed to measure it as follows [32]-

- Plot Titles, where participants are given the plot of a story and asked to write original titles.
- Quick Responses is a word-association test scored for uncommonness.
- Figure Concepts, where participants were given simple drawings of objects and individuals and asked to find qualities or features that are common in two or more drawings; these were scored for uncommonness.
- Unusual Uses is finding unusual uses for common everyday objects such as bricks.
- Remote Associations, where participants are asked to find a word between two given words (e.g. Hand _____ Call)
- Remote Consequences, where participants are asked to generate a list of consequences of unexpected events (e.g. loss of gravity)

Researchers who have attempted to measure creativity or creative aptitude use similar terms to describe it, including [33]:

- Fluency (number of ideas generated)
- Originality and imagination (unusual, unique, novel ideas)
- Elaboration (ability to explain ideas in detail)
- Flexibility, curiosity, resistance to closure (ability to generate multiple solutions)
- Complexity (detail and implications of ideas; recognition of patterns, similarities and differences)
- Risk taking (willingness to be wrong and to admit it)

Measuring can also be done by seeing if something looks right or feels right. This is synthesising significant amounts of experience and bringing it to bear on a new design or art work.

4.11 Barriers to Creativity

Business and the academy provide environments with a variety of cultures and practices. Some provide a framework which seeks to foster creativity and others do not. For example, in these situations there may be a reluctance to generate new ideas for fear of offending superiors, a reluctance to go beyond what the existing data actually state, or a lack of confidence that a valid new idea can be produced. Thus there can be a variety of psychological and cultural barriers to creativity, whether explicit or implicit. Organisations which are seeking to harness the benefits of creativity will seek to implement structures and ways of working that allow new ideas to be generated. Given that the academy has its roots in Plato's school of philosophy founded at Akademia, its objective is to learn, acquire knowledge, and extend the current boundaries of learning and scholarship. A key component of this is communication and openness, and a willingness to challenge existing traditions. Publication of research also enables the wider community to discuss and debate the latest advances.

Being able and willing to take risks is as much an integral part of art and design as it is for research and development in business.

4.12 Conditions for Creativity to Flourish

Nowotny [34] argues that while creativity needs certain conditions to flourish, it refuses to become subject to prediction.

Business organisations are often required to maximize business imperatives such as coordination, productivity, and control. These can have the effect of stifling creativity, which is often the key attribute needed in order to accomplish a substantive business development – either in product or process. However, creativity and business development can go hand in hand. It is not sufficient for a new idea to be original it must also be appropriate, useful and actionable. Amabile [35] has identified six managerial practices that can affect creativity. They are challenge, freedom, resources, work-group features, supervisory encouragement, and organizational support. Key aspects are openness and communication. Organisations that are open are the most likely to exhibit these characteristics. These categories resulted from more than two decades of research focused primarily on one question: what are the links between work environment and creativity?

The combination of structured and unstructured environments can be useful to ensure that there is maximum opportunity for new ideas to emerge. Organisations that value creative solutions generally provide employees with the freedom and motivation to think unhindered and to test out ideas without fear of being criticised or penalised.

4.13 Creativity and Big Data

Data gathering and data storage on a global basis is increasing at an exponential rate and doubling every 2 years. Global mobile data traffic is set to reach 52 petaabytes (PB) in 2015, an increase of 59 % from 2014, according to Gartner, Inc. The rapid growth is set to continue through 2018, when mobile data levels are estimated to reach 173 million TB. This raises the challenge of the significance of the data and how best to extract meaning from it in an optimum way. Clearly this can have significant implications for the data of a company and the relationship of the data to the performance of the company. This can be also relevant for design data and data produced in association with artistic processes. These also increasingly include social media data, where design or artistic collaborations are sharing views and information during the design process.

This massive increase in the volume of information being generated and circulated is analogous to that brought about by the printing press, and could thus constitute a new technological paradigm. However, extracting meaning and knowledge from very large data sets is a significant challenge often requiring multidisciplinary expertise of the kind provided by teams of mathematicians, statisticians, social scientists, data visualization specialists, and presentation experts.

Many corporations and research organisations are increasingly interested in extracting meaning from this data in order to improve their productivity and competitiveness. Powerful tools are needed to explore massive raw data and enable this to be done creatively to provide new and original ways of addressing such a complex problem. Searching for patterns in user data is now standard practice for many companies and organisations in order to understand current trends and potential future customer needs and requirements.

4.14 Creativity and Discovering the Unknown

Cook et al. [36] summarise the issues with exploring data to discover as yet unknown aspects about the data. Analytics can be used to reveals trends, patterns and associations. Visual analytics requires interdisciplinary science, which requires going beyond traditional scientific and information visualization to include statistics, mathematics, knowledge representation, management and discovery technologies, cognitive and perceptual sciences, and decision sciences. Presenting information in an accurate and meaningful way which is also easy to assimilate is often an area where artists and designers make significant contributions. The presentation and representation of the data has to be effective in conveying the information. It also has to convey the right information to the user and also decision-makers and not mislead some readers due to poor presentation design.

4.15 Percentage of GDP Spent by a Country on Research and Innovation

Creativity benefits from supportive environments. Research and innovation benefit people with ideas and the resources to support them. However, resources spent on research and development may not be an accurate predictor of productivity, the quality of the ideas produced, or economic growth. Nevertheless, analysing the percentage of GDP spent by countries on research and innovation shows significant differences. If the originality of the ideas is measured to some degree by the number of patents filed, those countries with a higher percentage of GDP allocated to research and innovation normally generate a larger number of patents. Thus percentage of GDP has a degree of correlation with original outputs.

4.16 Research in Creativity

Creativity is a multi-faceted and involves a large number of possible elements such as intellect, neurology, psychology, cognitive science, technology, business studies, economics, culture, and personality. Performing interdisciplinary research in these areas is a challenging task because in addition to research in each area, it is necessary consider the methods and practices in each area and also the boundary between the areas. In addition, there is a need for theoretical models which can be used to drive experimental investigations, and in turn be modified by them as new results come to light. Such models should help in the understanding of creative processes. Methods for measuring individual creativity are reviewed in Sect. 4.10. Companies and organisations are investing heavily in creating environments which support creativity in order to make a difference for their products and services in a competitive market place. Creative industries seek to utilise knowledge and information in order to generate new businesses. Traditionally, these involved the following creative sectors [37] –

1. Advertising and marketing
2. Architecture
3. Crafts
4. Design: product, graphic and fashion design
5. Film, TV, video, radio and photography
6. IT, software and computer services
7. Publishing
8. Museums, galleries and libraries
9. Music, performing and visual arts
10. Toys and games

Aspects of the education industry could also be included in this list. A distinction may be drawn between industries which have a potential for mass production and distribution (film and video, video games, broadcasting, publishing), and those that are primarily craft-based and are meant to be consumed in a particular place and context (visual arts, performing arts, cultural heritage). All these areas have the potential to contribute significantly to a nation's economic growth. This in turn depends on the quality of the creative ideas that are produced and how they are migrated into products and services that are attractive to consumers and address consumer needs and requirements.

4.17 Creativity and Paradigm Shift

Major changes in the status quo were characterised by Kuhn [38] as paradigm shifts. Although initially directed at scientific advances such as the Copernican revolution and the changes it accomplished in the understanding of the solar system and

Fig. 4.4 "Duck-Rabbit illusion". Licensed under Public Domain via Commons – https://commons.wikimedia.org/wiki/File:Duck-Rabbit_illusion.jpg#/media/File:Duck-Rabbit_illusion.jpg

the universe, it has since been generalised to cover all forms of the advancement of knowledge which cause significant changes in the world view. Although there is continuing debate on the extent of the change necessary to be classified as a paradigm shift, it is clear that such changes only come about by a mode of thinking that is outside the current world view. Such "thinking outside the box" is a characteristic of imagination and creativity.

Kuhn used the duck-rabbit optical illusion (Fig. 4.4) to demonstrate the way in which a paradigm shift could cause one to see the same information in an entirely different way.

What other changes could classify as paradigm shifts? The expansion of communication following the development of the printing press is a significant development. It also facilitated the expansion of learning by the increased dissemination of ideas and encouraged open publication and communication and the distribution of information.

The current avalanche of information, characterised as big data, represents a similar expansion of communication, particularly when such information can aggregate the views of millions of people by social media.

Dosi [39] and Perez [40] have contributed to the understanding of possible paradigm shifts associated with combinations of basic innovation, technical and institutional change, and economic development, and the links between innovation and financial dynamics.

It is possible that the digital environments of cyberworlds which bring substantially increased global collaboration and interaction will be seen over time to constitute a paradigm shift because of the significant changes they are able to accomplish to the traditional ways of thinking, working, interacting, and creating. Substantial developments in the area of creative industries indicate that radical and useful changes have been brought about by linking new knowledge and information to technological developments.

4.18 Conclusions

Creative processes are complex and multi-faceted. An idea in one area may provide the impetus for the generation of a new idea in another. Thus open ways of thinking and working may generate new concepts and ideas more readily than closed environments. The originality or usefulness of a new idea may not be immediately apparent; it may take time for its significance to be appreciated. One way of measuring the degree of originality is to observe how many other cognate lines of enquiry are generated with this as the starting point, or show many schools of thought or practice develop over time which are based in this initial concept. This may identify a concept or idea as 'ground-breaking'.

Analyses of research quality (Chap. 5) indicate that some research discoveries may be regarded as of higher value than others – by their innate merit, or the extent to which they constitute an advance in knowledge, or by the degree to which they have made an impact on the world.

The increase in digital environments provides opportunities for greater collaboration and online working. They also provide new opportunities for interaction and sharing of information across diverse groups of people. The design to manufacture life-cycle can be compressed in virtual environments, and also enable the end-to-end implications of design ideas and design changes to be more rapidly visualized and understood. These include visual appearance, environmental setting, internal and external usability, eco-issues, cost/benefit, functionality and performance evaluation.

New disciplines often arise at the boundaries between existing disciplines. Thus working in interdisciplinary areas may be a fruitful way forward, notwithstanding the challenges and difficulties this often entails. They also provide different perspectives on common problems or initiatives. These perspectives often reflect different cultures, contexts, traditions, and histories, which in turn can enhance the creative process.

Further Reading

Catmull, E.: Creativity, Inc.: Overcoming the Unseen Forces That Stand in the Way of True Inspiration, Bantam Press, p. 368, (2014)

De Bono, E.: Six Thinking Hats, Penguin, p. 192 (2009)

Lansdown, R.J., Earnshaw, R.A. (Eds.); Computers in Art, Design and Animation. Springer ISBN: 0-387-96896-2, p. 305 (1989)

Levoy, M.: Where Do Disruptive Ideas Come from? http://graphics.stanford.edu/~levoy/unc-commencement.html (2012)

Richards, R. (ed.): Everyday Creativity and New Views of Human Nature: Psychological, Social, and Spiritual Perspectives. APA, Washington, DC (2007)

Runco, M.A., Pritzker, S.: Encyclopedia of Creativity. Academic, San Diego (1999)

Sawyer, R.K.: Explaining Creativity: The Science of Human Innovation. Oxford University Press, New York (2006)

Thomas, K., Chan, J. (eds): Handbook of Research on Creativity, Edward Elgar Publications, pp 584, (2015)

The Science of Creativity. American Psychological Association http://www.apa.org/gradpsych/2009/01/creativity.aspx

References

1. Schnabel, M.A.: Architectural Design in Virtual Environments: Exploring Cognition and Communication in Immersive Virtual Environments, PhD Thesis, University of Hong Kong, http://cumincad.architexturez.net/system/files/pdf/2ccd.content.01425.pdf (2004)
2. Virtual Amusement Park (VPARK) http://cordis.europa.eu/project/rcn/46555_en.html
3. Joslin, C., Molet, T., Magnenat-Thalmann, N., Esmerado, J., Thalmann, D., Palmer, I.J., Chilton, N., Earnshaw, R.A.: Sharing attractions on the net with VPARK. IEEE Comput. Graph Appl. IEEE Comput. Soc. **21**(1), 61–71 (2001)
4. Virtual Interactive Studio Television Application using networked graphical supercomputers (VISTA) http://cordis.europa.eu/project/rcn/32297_en.html
5. Flerackers, C., Earnshaw, R.A., Vanischem, G., Van Reeth, F., Alsema, F.: Creating broadcast interactive drama in a networked virtual environment. IEEE Comput. Graph. Appl. **21**(1), 56–60 (2001)
6. Boden, M.: Can Computer Models Help Us to Understand Human Creativity? http://nationalhumanitiescenter.org/on-the-human/2010/05/can-computer-models-help-us-to-understand-human-creativity/
7. Boden, M.A.: The Creative Mind: Myths and Mechanisms. Weidenfeld and Nicholson, London (1990)
8. Boden, M.A. (ed.): Dimensions of Creativity. MIT Press, Cambridge, MA (1996)
9. Pearce, M.: Boden and Beyond: The Creative Mind and its Reception in the Academic Community http://webprojects.eecs.qmul.ac.uk/marcusp/notes/boden.pdf
10. Essinger, J.: Jacquard's Web: How a Hand Loom Led to the Birth of the Information Age, Oxford Universiy Press, p. 318 (2007)
11. Liggett, S., Heald, K., Earnshaw, R.A., Thompson, E., Excell, P.S.: Collaborative Research in Art, Design and New Media – Challenges and Opportunities, Proceedings of Internet Technologies and Applications (2015)
12. Earnshaw, R.A., Liggett S, Heald K.: Interdisciplinary Collaboration Methodologies in Art, Design and Media, Proceedings of International Conference on Internet Technologies and Applications, pp. 381–388, ISBN 978-0-946881-81-9, UK (2013)
13. Carroll, J. M. (Ed): Creativity and Rationale: Enhancing Human Experience by Design, Springer, p. 447. http://www.springer.com/us/book/9781447141105 (2013)
14. Google Acquires UK Artificial Intelligence Start-Up Deepmind, Guardian, http://www.theguardian.com/technology/2014/jan/27/google-acquires-uk-artificial-intelligence-startup-deepmind (2014)
15. Excell, P.S., Earnshaw, R.A.: The Future of Computing – The Implications for Society of Technology Forecasting and the Kurzweil Singularity, Proceedings of IEEE International Symposium on Technology and Society, Dublin, Ireland (2015)
16. Facing Experience: A Painter's Canvas in Virtual Reality, M. Dolinsky, PhD Thesis, Plymouth University, http://pearl.plymouth.ac.uk/handle/10026.1/32042014dolinsky304581phdAnnotated.pdf (2014)
17. Real vs Virtual: Examining Works of Art Online, D. Mack and H. E. Ojalvo, New York Times, February 7, 2011 http://learning.blogs.nytimes.com/2011/02/07/real-vs-virtual-examining-works-of-art-online/?_r=0

18. https://sites.google.com/site/ita15artexpoandworkshop/gallery
19. http://glyndwrpix.co.uk/carbonaugust2/
20. Online Collaboration: Scientists and the Social Network, R. van Noorden, Nature, 512, pp 126–129, 14 August 2014, doi:10.1038/512126a
21. Netscape Time: The Making of the Billion-dollar Start-up that Changed the World, J. Clark, St. Martin's Press, Inc, (1999)
22. Deloitte Mobile Consumer Survey 2015 http://www2.deloitte.com/uk/en/pages/technology-media-and-telecommunications/articles/mobile-consumer-survey.html
23. How Successful Virtual Teams Collaborate, K. Ferrazzi, Harvard Business Review, October 24, 2012 https://hbr.org/2012/10/how-to-collaborate-in-a-virtua
24. Crowd Accelerated Innovation, T. Curator, C. Anderson, Wired, 27 December 2010 http://www.wired.com/2010/12/ff_tedvideos/
25. Cunningham, S., Berry, D., Earnshaw, R.A., Excell, P.S.: Thompson E.: Multi-Disciplinary Creativity and Collaboration: Utilizing Crowd-Accelerated Innovation and the Internet, Proceedings of International Conference on Cyberworlds (CW2015), Sweden (2015)
26. Accelerating Innovation: The Power of the Crowd, KPMG https://www.kpmg.com/Ca/en/IssuesAndInsights/ArticlesPublications/Documents/Accelerating-Innovation-the-Power-of-the-Crowd.pdf
27. Brown, J.R., van Dam, A., Earnshaw, R.A., Encarnacao, J.L., Guedj, R.A.: Human-centered computing, online communities and virtual environments. IEEE Comput. Graph. Appl. **19**(6), 70–74 (1999)
28. Brown, J.R., van Dam, A., Earnshaw, R.A., Encarnacao, J.L., Guedj, R.A.: Special report on human-centered computing, online communities and virtual environments. ACM SIGGRAPH Comput. Graph ACM **33**(3), 42–62 (1999)
29. Earnshaw, R.A. Guedj, R.A., van Dam, A., Vince, J.A.: Frontiers of Human-Centered Computing, Online Communities and Virtual Environments, Springer-Verlag, pp 482, ISBN: 1-85233-238-7 (2001)
30. Asimov, I.: Isaac Asimov Asks How Do People Get New Ideas? MIT Technology Review, 20 October (2014)
31. Guildford, J. P.: The Nature of Human Intelligence, McGraw-Hill, pp 538, (1967)
32. https://en.wikipedia.org/wiki/Creativity#Assessing_individual_creative_ability
33. http://www.celt.iastate.edu/teaching-resources/classroom-practice/teaching-techniques-strategies/creativity/defining-creativity/
34. Nowotny, H.: The Cunning of Uncertainty, Polity, p. 220 (2015)
35. Amabile, T.: How to Kill Creativity, Harvard Business Review, Sept/Oct 1998. https://hbr.org/1998/09/how-to-kill-creativity/ar/1 (1998)
36. Cook, K.A., Earnshaw, R.A., Stasko, J.: Discovering the unexpected. IEEE. Comput. Graph. Appl. IEEE. Comput. Soc. **27**(5), 15–19 (2007). http://www.computer.org/csdl/mags/cg/2007/05/mcg2007050015-abs.html
37. https://en.wikipedia.org/wiki/Creative_industries
38. Kuhn, T. S.: The Structure of Scientific Revolutions, University of Chicago Press, (originally published 1962) (1996)
39. Mazzucato, M.: Giovanni Dosi, Innovation, Organization and Economic Dynamics: Selected Essays, Edward Elgar Publishing, Cheltenham, UK/Northampton, MA, pp. X+703, (2000)
40. Perez, C.: Technological Revolutions and Financial Capital: The Dynamics of Bubbles and Golden Ages. Elgar, London (2002)

Chapter 5
Research Monitoring and Audit in Art and Design

Abstract Periodic assessment of research in UK universities has taken place since 1986. This is used as a case study in order to highlight the key issues involved in monitoring and auditing of research. The most recent audit in the UK took place during 2014 with the results being published at the end of 2014. This case study is concerned with art and design though all disciplines were included in the national assessment. The method used for assessing research quality is outlined and the results summarised. Primarily this was by means of peer review of published research outputs by a panel of leading experts in the area, with international experts to ensure parity with international standards. Other factors used were the impact of the work being submitted and the quality of the research environment where the work had been done. The standing of the vehicle of publication was not used as a proxy for the quality of the publication, though citation data was used in some areas to confirm evaluations. Practice-led and practice-based research have also generated substantial discussion in terms of seeking a consensus on what is appropriate for developmental purposes and academic assessment. In addition, this area also needs evaluation methods which are fair and consistent across different types of practice. The lessons drawn from the evaluation by the UK Research Excellence Framework in 2014 are detailed. A comparison of peer review methods with the use of bibliometrics is presented. A number of issues are identified and discussed. These include the staff selected for submission, the method of evaluation, and a cost-benefit analysis of the process.

Keywords Research assessment • Quality profile • Research outputs • Research impact • Knowledge transfer • Research environment • Practice-based research • Interdisciplinarity • Creative disciplines • Metrics • Research monitoring

5.1 Introduction

The UK has had periodic research evaluation exercises from 1986 onwards, and approximately every 5 years, on behalf of the four UK higher education funding councils (HEFCE, SHEFC, HEFCW, DELNI). Submissions from each subject area (or "unit of assessment") were given a quality ranking by a subject specialist peer review panel composed of experts in the field. The rankings were used to inform the allocation of quality weighted research funding (QR) that higher education institutions might receive (if their outcomes were above a threshold) from their national funding council for each of the years between research assessments [1]. The UK uses a dual funding mechanism to support research – QR and direct application for grants. QR funding is done at an institutional level (though this is normally passed on to the research group earning it). The Research Councils also receive applications for grants from individual researchers, or groups of researchers, which are then peer reviewed. The submissions receiving the highest ratings receive grant funding.

Over time the formula for allocation of QR has resulted in the funding becoming more selective. Following the assessment in 2008, the ratio of the subsequent QR funding allocation across 4*, 3*, 2*, and 1* rankings was 7:3:1:0. From 2012 the ranking of 2* no longer received any financial allocation, so funding was limited to those areas with 4* and 3* rankings and the ratio of funding was 3:1. This has raised the issue of institutions having research areas that are funded by the QR they have earned, and other research areas not submitted, or which resulted in scores below 3*, having no QR to fund them. The question has been raised whether such research is economically viable given the increasing competitive nature of research at national and international levels, and the increasing selectivity brought about the limiting of QR funding to only the highest levels of quality (4* and 3*).

It was replaced by the Research Excellence Framework (REF) in 2014, though the method of assessment has produced similar results to those in earlier evaluations. The funding formula for QR following REF2014 was announced as 4:1 (ratio of 4* to 3*) by the UK funding council in February 2015, and determines the distribution of approximately £1.6 billion of research funding annually from the UK funding councils starting with 2015–2016. Thus selectivity in funding has been increased though it has been argued that because of the overall rise in 4* and 3* research, the changing of the ratio for funding would have minimum effect.

In the UK, the evaluation of research outputs is done for each individual in a submission. However, the results are published in collective form. Thus it is not possible to identify the scores achieved by a particular individual, unless the number of staff in a submission is very small (in which case some guesses could be made). Instead, the results are published as a profile for all the staff in the submission corresponding to a particular unit of assessment from an institution.

In 2010, Excellence in Research for Australia (ERA) used two databases containing all the known publication vehicles for conferences and journals [2]. The rankings were produced by the Australian Research Council (ARC) in consultation with members of the public, expert reviewers and academic bodies. This list included quality ranks for each journal. Ranked journal publishing profiles were used as part of the suite of indicators in the ERA 2010 evaluation. Following feedback from the Research Evaluation Committees that they relied on their own expert knowledge of the quality of research outlets relevant to their discipline, ranked journal profiles were removed as an indicator for the ERA 2012 evaluation.

5.1 Introduction

Table 5.1 ERA rating scale for 2010

Rating	Descriptor
5	The Unit of Evaluation profile is characterised by evidence of outstanding performance **well above world standard** presented by the suite of indicators used for evaluation
4	The Unit of Evaluation profile is characterised by evidence of performance **above world standard** presented by the suite of indicators used for evaluation
3	The Unit of Evaluation profile is characterised by evidence of average performance **at world standard** presented by the suite of indicators used for evaluation
2	The Unit of Evaluation profile is characterised by evidence of performance **below world standard** presented by the suite of indicators used for evaluation
1	The Unit of Evaluation profile is characterised by evidence of performance **well below world standard** presented by the suite of indicators used for evaluation
n/a	Not assessed due to low volume. The number of research outputs does not meet the volume threshold standard for evaluation in ERA

http://archive.arc.gov.au/archive_files/ERA/2010/Key%20Documents/ERA_rating_scale.pdf

This produced a ranked list on the scale A*, A, B, C, D and Not Ranked (Table 5.1). This corresponded approximately to the quality levels used in the UK.

Using these databases, the evaluation of publications could have become a mechanistic process with the ranking of the publications being determined by the ranking of their publication vehicles. Possible weaknesses could include the following –

- Lack of full agreement by those being assessed on the rankings of the publication vehicles
- If the ranking of a particular journal or conference proceedings was incorrect, then this could affect the evaluation of all papers appearing in these publications
- Higher quality papers appearing in lower quality (i.e. ranked) publication vehicles could be undervalued (and vice-versa)
- The degree of correlation between publication vehicle rank and paper rank may not be same for all disciplines, and may vary over time
- Some disciplines (e.g. art, design and media), where the published outputs tend to be in non-standard form, do not fit easily into a method which uses quantitative metrics
- Influence on the behaviour of those being assessed – as it could cause researchers to then only target the highest ranked journals and conferences, which could have a distorting effect on the field and its publishers

Further consideration resulted in these databases not being used after 2011, and a range of metrics is now used including citation profiles of papers and peer review. The data submitted by universities includes all eligible researchers, and the indicators used have been developed in close consultation with the research community [3]. It is also aimed to minimise the resourcing burden of ERA for Government and universities that is required for the research assessment.

5.2 Assessing Research Quality

5.2.1 Research Quality

The primary criteria used in the evaluation of research quality in REF2014 were "*originality, significance and rigour*" [4]. In general, these are accepted internationally as key measures of research excellence. These criteria were used to assess the quality of the research outputs (generally the four works submitted for full-time faculty for the period 1 January 2008 to 31 December 2013). Research outputs contributed 65 % to the overall quality profile. Further components in the evaluation were the impact at 20 % (based on a selected number of submitted case studies) and environment at 15 % (based on the characteristics of the area in the institution where the research was done) [4]. Impact was a new category introduced in this assessment and, prior to the publication of the outcomes, was the subject of considerable discussion and also disagreement on the part of researchers; subsequently, the criticisms have been much more muted.

Knowledge transfer has already made considerable advances in the UK and internationally [5]. As economies advance it is argued that they migrate from resource-based to knowledge-based production. Thus knowledge and innovation are two of the factors behind job creation and economic growth. This in turn affects the social context and also public and economic policy. Many national governments have therefore sought to address the challenges implicit in this observation and, in particular, provide motivation and incentives to increase the collaboration between industry and the academy in the expectation that there will be direct benefits to a nation's economy and overall global competitiveness. In turn, the academy has sought to address the challenges and opportunities where they align with their institutional mission. Clark [6] used the phrase "*entrepreneurial universities*" to characterize the aspects of promoting technology transfer within national systems of learning and innovation.

Whether public or private, industry increasingly seeks to use tools and techniques that increase efficiency and effectiveness, whilst at the same time maximizing quality and minimizing cost. The current trend towards companies outsourcing their R & D requirements to reduce corporate overheads and optimize staffing levels means that Universities can utilize the opportunity and bid to supply this expertise. Universities also generate their own spin-outs from intellectual property they create, as well as licensing technology to industry, rather than transferring it.

Knowledge transfer is therefore one aspect of the impact of research. Although art and design may not generate as many patents as the applied sciences, there are significant areas of creativity and design that can have a major impact on products and services. For example, Apple is noted for the attention paid to the detailed aspects of the design of products, their user interfaces, and their usability. In addition, exhibitions and museums also contribute substantially to the cultural context of nations.

5.2.2 Research Outputs

Research outputs in the majority of the discipline areas were predominantly publications in the peer reviewed literature. It is generally accepted that the extent of the peer reviewing involved in such publications may contribute in some degree to an indication of their quality. However, neither the impact factor of the researcher nor the impact factor of the publication vehicle were formally taken into account in the evaluation. The publication was evaluated by a number of expert reviewers on the panel and then ranked by agreement across the reviewers. However, it is clear that it would be difficult for such reviewers to be unaware of the status of the researcher or the publication vehicle, as blind reviewing was not used. Subject panels had international representation for the purposes of benchmarking the UK evaluation.

In creative discipline areas, the types of research outputs accepted as valid were much wider [7]. As set out in Chap. 1, outputs could include (and were not limited to) the following [4] –

- books (authored or edited)
- chapters in books
- journal articles
- working papers
- published conference papers
- electronic resources and publications
- exhibition or museum catalogues
- translations; scholarly editions
- creative writing and compositions
- curatorship and conservation
- databases
- grammars
- dictionaries
- digital and broadcast media
- performances and other types of live presentation
- artefacts
- designs and exhibitions
- films, videos and other types of media presentation
- software design and development
- advisory report
- the creation of archival or specialist collections to support the research infrastructure.

In addition, all types of research or forms of output, whether they were physical or virtual, textual or non-textual, visual or sonic, static or dynamic, digital or analogue, were all equally acceptable and none had any advantage over the other. All forms of output were evaluated using methods appropriate to the form of output.

Table 5.2 Outputs sub-profile: criteria and definitions of starred levels

Ranking	Specification
Four star	Quality that is world-leading in terms of originality, significance and rigour
Three star	Quality that is internationally excellent in terms of originality, significance and rigour but which falls short of the highest standards of excellence
Two star	Quality that is recognised internationally in terms of originality, significance and rigour
One star	Quality that is recognised nationally in terms of originality, significance and rigour
Unclassified	Quality that falls below the standard of nationally recognised work. Or work which does not meet the published definition of research for the purposes of this assessment

The ranking of each output was according to the definitions in Table 5.2. These rankings were then included in a profile distribution of all outputs within a particular submission. Thus it is not possible to determine from the published results which output (and therefore which member of staff) contributed to each rank. In this sense therefore, the results are essentially anonymised. However, if a submission only contained a small number of people, then it could be possible to identify which person contributed to high ranked outputs and which to low rankings – as all the outputs (i.e. the reference data for the published paper or book) are included in the published results for REF2014. One exception is where an output contained information of commercial sensitivity which was submitted in confidence by the institution and which was then evaluated in confidence. Not to be able to include such work would have disadvantaged institutions with significant commercial contracts and where it was not possible to publish the results of the work in the open literature. In addition, it made it clear that research leading to commercial outputs could be regarded as of the same standing as pure research and would be evaluated according to the same criteria.

The criteria for assessing the quality of outputs are 'originality, significance and rigour' as summarised in Table 5.2 [4].

5.2.3 Research Impact

Attention in recent years by funding bodies has not only been on research, but also on assessing the extent to which the results of the research have subsequently been utilised by companies, public bodies, and the wider society beyond the academy. This could be expressed in terms of the beneficial impact on industry, particularly if the research has led to new patents, products, processes or procedures which have improved business efficiency and effectiveness or improved the position of UK businesses in world markets, or else verifiable social benefits in health, well-being, employment, etc. Such assessment of impact was not confined to business

5.2 Assessing Research Quality

Table 5.3 Indicative range of impacts

Area	Description
Civil society	Informing and influencing the form and content of associations between people or groups to illuminate and challenge cultural values and social assumptions
Cultural life	Creating and interpreting cultural capital in all of its forms to enrich and expand the lives, imaginations and sensibilities of individuals and groups
Economic prosperity	Applying and transferring the insights and knowledge gained from research to create wealth in the manufacturing, service, creative and cultural sectors
Education	Informing and influencing the form or the content of the education of any age group in any part of the world where they extend significantly beyond the submitting Higher Education Institution
Policy making	Informing and influencing policy debate and practice through interventions relating to any aspect of human or animal well-being or the environment
Public discourse	Extending the range and improving the quality of evidence, argument and expression to enhance public understanding of the major issues and challenges faced by individuals and society
Public services	Contributing to the development and delivery of public services or legislation to support the welfare, education, understanding or empowerment of diverse individuals and groups in society, including the disadvantaged or marginalised

or industry but included all forms of societal and cultural value. The latter have special relevance for the arts and humanities, particularly in the area of practice-led research.

The REF2014 document on the Criteria to be used in the evaluation of research included the following information on the indicative range of impacts (Table 5.3).

The evaluation of impact [4] was done using the case studies and measured the degree of reach and significance of the work included in each of the case studies submitted. This implies that the research outputs included within each case study had to have a degree of applicability to, and recognition by, one or more aspects of the wider business and societal environment. Thus for art and design, such case studies included creative works in a variety of forms including exhibitions, installations, applications, media works, collaborations, etc. The case studies had to have a research content of at a rank of at least 2*. Again the results are anonymised since it is not possible to determine the score for a particular case study (unless only one was submitted). Thus there is no opportunity to challenge the evaluation subsequently.

The ranking of the impact in the case studies was according to the definitions in Table 5.4.

Previous research assessments did not include impact per se, but used a less verifiable concept of 'esteem', which may be said to equate to direct and indirect measures of impact such as could be accomplished by evaluating such aspects as patents, citations in news media, industrial recognition, and economic significance.

Table 5.4 Impact sub-profile: criteria and definitions of starred levels

Ranking	Specification
Four star	Outstanding impacts in terms of their reach and significance
Three star	Very considerable impacts in terms of their reach and significance
Two star	Considerable impacts in terms of their reach and significance
One star	Recognised but modest impacts in terms of their reach and significance
Unclassified	The impact is of little or no reach and significance; or the impact was not eligible; or the impact was not underpinned by excellent research produced by the submitted unit

To provide greater externality at REF2014, evaluations of impact in art and design were also performed by key representatives of local government, publishing, arts non-governmental organisations, the design industries and the public museum service. However, it is still not certain how accurate or useful such measures are when determining the longer term value of research, particularly pure research, when the measurement is done on a short term basis. However, this point has been raised in the context of discussions about future assessments, where it could be possible to track how far these same areas have increased their impact over time, essentially giving a longer time frame for overall assessment. This could provide an evaluation of the degree to which a particular piece of research had provided a major impact on the field.

5.2.4 Research Environment

With regard to the research environment, the reviewers assessed this in terms of its vitality and sustainability [4] including its contribution to the vitality and sustainability of the wider discipline or research base. The ranking of research environment was according to the definitions in Table 5.5.

5.2.5 Interdisciplinary Research

Criteria used to measure research quality generally focus on a particular research area (called the Unit of Assessment). These are the subject and discipline areas where the research takes place. This immediately poses a challenge for appropriately assessing interdisciplinary research which may contain two or more discipline areas. These areas often combine the arts and science, the arts and technology, or the arts and medicine, where the value of the research outputs may be viewed differently in each of the contributing disciplines. How to truly reconcile these differences and produce a fair and appropriate evaluation is difficult, and has been recognised for some time in the evaluation of interdisciplinary research grant proposals. For

5.3 Results of the Evaluation

Table 5.5 Environment sub-profile: criteria and definitions of starred levels

Ranking	Specification
Four star	An environment that is conducive to producing research of world-leading quality, in terms of its vitality and sustainability
Three star	An environment that is conducive to producing research of internationally excellent quality, in terms of its vitality and sustainability
Two star	An environment that is conducive to producing research of internationally recognised quality, in terms of its vitality and sustainability
One star	An environment that is conducive to producing research of nationally recognised quality, in terms of its vitality and sustainability
Unclassified	An environment that is not conducive to producing research of nationally recognised quality

example, it has been common in the latter for reviewers in one discipline to not fully understand the contribution of the other discipline(s) and negatively evaluate the overall proposal. The method chosen by REF2014 panels was to cross-refer specific parts of a submission between sub-panels corresponding to the subject areas in an output. The Overview Panel Report for Panel D, Unit of Assessment 34 [8], indicated that only 3.7 % of the outputs were cross-referred outside Panel D and these were evaluated in the external sub-panel by the criteria of Panel D and not the criteria of the particular sub-panel to which they were referred. However, the extent to which this was successful is not known. It is also not known how many interdisciplinary research outputs were not submitted by institutions because fear that a low rating of this work could negatively affect their overall profile scores.

5.3 Results of the Evaluation

The submissions and the results for Art and Design were published online [9, 10]. The Times Higher Education lists the results by the overall performance of institutions and also by subject [11]. Table 5.6 gives the average profiles for the ranking categories for all the submissions in art and design [12].

Summary data for art and design (all submissions)

Number of submissions	84
Category A FTE staff submitted	1604
Category A and C staff submitted	2027
Career researchers	301
No of outputs submitted	6356
No of case studies submitted	239

The profile of outputs is not untypical of other disciplines. However, the scores for both impact and environment are significantly higher than those for outputs

Table 5.6 Average sub-profiles (%) for all submissions in art and design (FTE weighted) [10]

	4*	3*	2*	1*	U/C
Overall	26	42	25	6	1
Outputs	18.5	42.6	30	7.7	1.2
Impact	36.6	44.7	13.6	3.9	1.2
Environment	40.5	40.8	15.5	3	0.2

in the 4* category. Similar differences occurred in most disciplines. The overall impact across all disciplines scored an average of 3.24 (out of 4) compared with an average of 2.90 for outputs. One possible cause of this is that as the case studies were only four pages long, they were easier to assess. A further possibility is that some reviewers of case studies could have graded more leniently than for outputs in order to seek to influence funders and politicians in favour of their discipline [13]. Many of the outputs as published papers containing the detailed results of research would take a substantial amount of review time. This in turn would give more scope for reviewers to find questions or issues with regard to the published work and, if in doubt, mark it down a grade.

However, it has been noted that one case study was required for every ten faculty submitted, so the lower number of case studies submitted compared to outputs could give a higher margin for error. The difference between a 4* and a 3* rating for one case study could be significant in terms of its overall effect on the grade. In addition, those submissions with a larger number of faculty had more scope to demonstrate quality case studies. It can also be noted that because the scores for impact and environment show a wider variation than for outputs, they count more than their specified weighting in determining the overall score. On this basis impact counted overall for 29 % (rather than 20 %) and outputs 47 % (rather than 65 %) across all disciplines. This also explains the large numbers of REF submissions across all subjects that contain staff numbers just below the threshold required for submitting an extra case study. This could have had a distorting effect not only on the results of the REF, but also on the future careers of those staff who were excluded. In other words, what is being measured may not reflect the reality on the ground in the institution in terms of overall research culture and research strength. This could be used as an argument in future to require the inclusion of all eligible staff in the submission for assessment, which would avoid strategies that institutions clearly adopted with regard to the numbers of staff included, in an attempt to optimise the position of the institution and its discipline areas in league tables.

The results of the highest performing submissions in art and design are shown in Table 5.7 when ranked according to grade point average [11].

One way of making the results more representative of the areas being measured is to multiply the Grade Point Average (GPA) by the number of staff submitted, producing a measure of research volume. However, it has been argued that this favours large departments (who may have still omitted staff from the submission) and a more accurate measure would be to use the proportion of eligible staff submitted. This multiplies the GPA of the profile scores by the proportion of staff

5.4 Lessons from the Overview Reports

Table 5.7 Rank order by GPA in art and design

Rank order	Institution	FTE staff	% of 4*	GPA	Research power
1	Reading B	8	56	3.51	29
2	Courtauld	33	56	3.49	113
3	Westminster	24	45	3.36	81
4	St Andrews	13	38	3.30	42
5	York	19	47	3.29	62
6	Manchester	12	42	3.26	37
7	Ulster	25	47	3.24	80
=8	Sheffield Hallam	24	42	3.22	79
=8	UCL A	17	37	3.22	55
10	Essex	5	32	3.21	15
11	Warwick	11	40	3.19	35
12	Soas	10	35	3.16	31
13	Leeds A	16	34	3.15	49
14	Open	23	29	3.13	73
=15	Arts London	110	31	3.10	342

submitted (i.e. dividing the number of staff submitted by the actual total number of staff eligible). This is termed research power or research intensity, and seeks to make the research strength in depth in a department more explicit. This measure has been calculated and published in league tables by various bodies and is included in Table 5.7. Full tables have been published using this methodology to determine the rank order of institutions [13] in contrast to Table 5.7 which uses GPA to determine rank order. The results are broadly comparable with Table 5.7 but it does cause some institutions to drop out of the top 15 where the proportion of submitted staff (compared to total eligible staff) was relatively low. It also caused others to enter the higher rankings where the reverse was the case.

The number of PhDs completed may be used as a measure of research culture, though other factors could be used such as total research and contract income for the period. It can be argued that PhD completions also includes an element of impact since the training received by PhD students is then used by them subsequently in a variety of external contexts beyond their original training. The well-established centres for Art and Design in the UK did well on both PhD completions and also total research income (Table 5.8).

5.4 Lessons from the Overview Reports

The overview report from the sub-panel responsible for art and design detailed a number of the significant features of the submissions [8]. These are summarised below in three categories – strengths, weaknesses, and observations.

Table 5.8 Results for art and design with highest numbers of PhD completions, 2008–2013

Institution	Staff submitted FTE	Impact case studies	PhDs awarded 2008–2013	Total research income 2008–2013 (million)
Courtauld Institute of Art	32.5	4	84	£5.747
Royal College of Art	59.55	7	57	£6.848
UCL	36	6	42	£0.404
Univ of the Arts	109.7	12	63	£8.011
Goldsmiths	31.3	4	48	£3.848
Loughborough	54.73	6	87	£11.162

5.4.1 Strengths

There was an increased proportion of innovative and productive interdisciplinary research compared to 2008, particularly within areas of product and digital design, film, curatorship, media studies, conceptual and performance-based art practice. The majority of the interdisciplinarity resulted from collaborations with disciplines outside art and design and included engineering, physical sciences, computer science, health, medical, languages, drama, dance and performing arts. Practice-based research is a key feature of art and design and the submissions confirmed that the sector is a leader in this area of research activity, and in the elaboration of emergent approaches to knowledge. There was also growth at the interface between traditional practice and the innovative use of digital technology. Collaboration between practitioners and museums has led to advances in archival environments. Exhibitions and conservation studies were evident across all subject areas and demonstrated strength.

5.4.2 Weaknesses

The intellectual and theoretical underpinning of graphic and communication design was regarded as weak. There was evaluative commentary on esteem, impact and status of the outputs, such as by reviews and publicity materials, rather than providing an explanation of the significance of the research. This was felt to be a deficiency. Some of the output portfolios contained highly disparate materials without explanation or elaboration, which again was regarded as weak.

5.4.3 Observations

Contemporary art featured prominently as expected. However, art history outputs showed the continuing importance of work in earlier periods including Byzantine, Medieval and Renaissance studies. Cross-cultural and interdisciplinary studies reflected a dynamic expansion of the frontiers of the discipline. All forms of publications (books, journals, etc.) comprised 57 % of the outputs across art history and art and design practice, whereas artefacts only comprised 11 %. There was an increased range of exhibition activity compared to 2008, including museums, galleries, festivals and local authorities. Social and economic impact of the work was substantial with 81 % being judged at the highest quality levels. In addition, 81 % of the research environment described by submitted institutions was judged to be world-leading and/or internationally excellent. Some institutions had obtained large amounts of funding during the period and had also been very successful in large numbers of PhD completions.

5.4.4 Discussion

A number of points arise from this consideration. These include the extent to which the assessment is representative of an area in an institution, given that all academic staff within the area are not included because each institution makes a selection to seek to get the best result, other methods of evaluation, the cost effectiveness of the evaluation, and opportunities lost due to the time and money spent on the evaluation. These points would apply to all disciplines in the assessment, not just art and design. In areas where art and design raise separate issues with regard to the points raised these are noted.

5.5 Staff Selection

The selective inclusion of staff, as noted earlier, can have a distorting effect not only on the results of the REF, but it can also on the future careers of those staff who were excluded. In other words, what is being measured is only a sub-section of a department or institution. A measure such as research power (Sect. 5.3) may be of more interest to potential PhD students or potential members of staff, and even funding bodies. This could be used as an argument to support the inclusion of all eligible staff in future submissions.

5.6 Use of Metrics

It has been observed from the start of periodic research assessments that other parameters could be used to measure research quality, including research grants, individual and departmental H-index, and PhD completions. The advantage of these is that their data is already available in institutional or national databases and would not involve the generation of any new data (which costs time and money). Research grants are peer reviewed and are increasingly competitive, so this element of peer review is already in the system. An early evaluation was done in a previous RAE on research grants alone for an engineering area, and the difference between the rankings obtained by detailed review of outputs as in REF2014 compared to the ranking based on research grants alone was less than 0.1 %. In the past, using this proxy has been resisted because there was no research council to award grants in the arts and humanities, but now there is – and so this argument is weakened. Also, it is recognised that significant advances in the arts and humanities may be less dependent on large grants since there is less dependence on research laboratories and high-cost specialist equipment. An individual's H-index measures both the productivity and citation impact of a person's body of work and is therefore much more wide-ranging than just selecting the best four publications. It has been argued that this metric favours more mature scholars who have been able to build up a substantial body of work over time and therefore younger scholars fare less well on this metric. However, it is the same situation for everyone in all the submissions. It has also been argued that overall it probably gives a more accurate assessment of the quality of published work than, say, two panel members reading four publications of a scholar and then giving these a score. If the original papers were submitted to an international journal, they would probably have been more widely read and assessed by international reviewers before publication than they were in the REF. Thus the refereeing process is essentially being duplicated when it is known to be prone to possible differing judgements, or even errors, if the expertise of the panel reviewer is not sufficiently close to the research area of the publication [14, 15]. This is particularly critical at the 4*/3* and 3*/2* boundaries simply because of the potential financial implications. Since 2* research is no longer funded any output ranked below 3* will receive no funding. The anonymity of the audit process and the results prevents the panel members coming under subsequent scrutiny or legal challenge if their evaluation of a publication differs significantly from what the previous reviewing prior to publication had indicated. The proportion of outputs that were scored differently to their ratings when originally reviewed for publication is not known – as the scores produced by the panels is kept confidential to the panel. There is a similar situation with regard to the measurement of impact in the case studies. These are aggregated so it is not possible to determine the rank given for a particular case study. This lack of full openness and transparency in the evaluation of outputs and case studies is out of synchronisation with the requirements of modern methods of public assessment. Using a departmental H-index (rather than individual) would be equivalent to issuing the results in profile form, and would preserve anonymity, if this requirement were to continue.

Preliminary results have already been published comparing the use of metrics (e.g. such as the Departmental or Research Group H-index for a particular research area) with the results of the peer reviewed research assessments in the UK at 2008 and 2014. For the latter, more work is still to be done but initial results present a fair degree of overall correlation between the use of metrics and the results published from REF2014 in core science and technology areas [16].

5.7 Use of Metrics in Art and Design

It has been noted that the use of H-index in the arts and humanities is less well-accepted, simply because the nature of publication is different. For example, the wide variety of outputs at varying time intervals does not lend itself to citation to the same extent as the more regular and more incremental publications in science and engineering. However, it was noted in Sect. 5.4.3 that in the outputs submitted to the REF, 57 % corresponded to traditional forms of publication (books, journals, etc.), whereas artefacts only comprised 11 %. Thus it is possible for the 57 % to be evaluated by means of metrics to some extent; with the remainder being evaluated by a peer review process.

In the arts and humanities there may be a weaker correlation between metrics such as paper citation count or journal impact factor and the results of the peer review process by a panel of experts in the field. Possible reasons for this could include the following factors – publication is via many different forms and media; journal impact factors and citations rates are not yet fully accepted as a proxy for quality in the arts and humanities; half-lives of publications tend to be much longer than in science and technology; and monographs, works of art, and compositions may be more important from the fifteenth century than a recent secondary source [17, 18]. In science and technology, the latter is normally unlikely to be the case. Peer review processes in these areas generally check first of all that all the relevant and most recent work is cited in a publication to give confidence that the research published may be regarded as a new and distinctive advance on current knowledge.

A counter-argument is that for books and monographs there is a case for the academic standing and reputation of the publisher to be used as a proxy for quality – since there can be a demonstrated link between a rigorous editorial review process using reviewers of international standing, and the degree of originality, rigour and significance of the work being submitted for publication. These characteristics are generally accepted internationally as a measure of research quality and degree of excellence, and were used as the primary criteria for assessing research outputs at REF2014 [19]. These were augmented at RAE2008 with an evaluation of the esteem factors of the researcher including recognition, influence and benefit. At REF2014 these have been replaced in part by Impact Case Studies. In addition, for books and monographs, Libcitations [20] has been proposed as an additional measure of value based on library data as an instrument for gauging the cultural significance and impact of books.

5.8 Review of Metrics by the Higher Education Funding Council

HEFCE carried out an independent review of the role of metrics in research assessment. The main findings of the review include the following [21]:

- *There is considerable scepticism among researchers, universities, representative bodies and learned societies about the broader use of metrics in research assessment and management.*
- *Peer review, despite its flaws, continues to command widespread support as the primary basis for evaluating research outputs, proposals and individuals. However, a significant minority are enthusiastic about greater use of metrics, provided appropriate care is taken.*
- *Carefully selected indicators can complement decision-making, but a 'variable geometry' of expert judgement, quantitative indicators and qualitative measures that respect research diversity will be required.*
- *There is legitimate concern that some indicators can be misused or 'gamed': journal impact factors, university rankings and citation counts being three prominent examples.*
- *The data infrastructure that underpins the use of metrics and information about research remains fragmented, with insufficient interoperability between systems.*
- *Analysis concluded that that no metric can currently provide a like-for-like replacement for REF peer review.*
- *In assessing research outputs in the REF, it is not currently feasible to assess research outputs or impacts in the REF using quantitative indicators alone.*
- *In assessing impact in the REF, it is not currently feasible to use quantitative indicators in place of narrative case studies. However, there is scope to enhance the use of data in assessing research environments.*

The review identified 20 recommendations for further work and action by stakeholders across the UK research system. They propose action in the following areas: supporting the effective leadership, governance and management of research cultures; improving the data infrastructure that supports research information management; increasing the usefulness of existing data and information sources; using metrics in the next REF; and coordinating activity and building evidence.

These recommendations are underpinned by the notion of 'responsible metrics' as a way of framing appropriate uses of quantitative indicators in the governance, management and assessment of research. Responsible metrics can be understood in terms of the following dimensions:

- **Robustness**: *basing metrics on the best possible data in terms of accuracy and scope*
- **Humility**: *recognising that quantitative evaluation should support – but not supplant – qualitative, expert assessment*
- **Transparency**: *keeping data collection and analytical processes open and transparent, so that those being evaluated can test and verify the results*
- **Diversity**: *accounting for variation by field, and using a range of indicators to reflect and support a plurality of research and researcher career paths across the system*
- **Reflexivity**: *recognising and anticipating the systemic and potential effects of indicators, and updating them in response.*

5.9 Evaluation of the UK Research Excellence Framework 2014

HEFCE has also set up a number projects to evaluate REF 2014 and to inform policy development for future audits [16]. This review includes an evaluation of impact of research, assessing multidisciplinary and interdisciplinary research, and the cost of the REF.

A Review of estimated costs of REF 2014 has been published [3] and includes the following key costs –

> *The total cost to the UK of running REF 2014 is estimated to be £246 M. That comprises around £232 M in costs to the higher education (HE) community and around £14 M in costs for the four UK higher education funding bodies.*

> *The cost to the HE community comprised around £212 M for the submission process and around £19 M for panellists' time. The £212 M cost of preparing the REF submissions comprises an element for preparing impact submissions, £55 M, and an element for all other costs incurred by HEIs, £157 M . . . .*

> *The REF assessed the outputs and impact of HEI research supported by many types of funders. In the context of £27bn total research income from public sources in the UK over a six-year period, the £246 M total cost for REF 2014 is less than 1%. In the context of dual support, the total cost amounts to roughly 2.4% of the £10.2 billion in research funds expected to be distributed by the UK's funding bodies in the six years, 2015–16 to 2020–21. This compares with an estimate of the annual cost to the UK HE community for peer review of grant applications of around £196 M or around 6% of the funds distributed by the Research Councils*

It is not clear whether the opportunity cost for higher education institution staff preparing the REF submission has been fully evaluated or take into account. The cost is not just the staff time, but the loss in research that could have been done in the year or more that most institutions spent on REF matters.

5.10 Distinctive Considerations for Creative Disciplines

There have always been distinctive qualitative differences between the policies of the assessors of UK university research covering creative disciplines, as opposed to the majority that might be characterised as analytical disciplines. The creative disciplines can succinctly be listed (using the groupings applying for the 2014 exercise) as:

- English Language and Literature
- Art and Design: History, Practice and Theory
- Music, Drama, Dance and Performing Arts
- Communication, Cultural and Media Studies, Library and Information Management

Within these disciplines it has become accepted practice that created artefacts can be considered as "research outputs", reflecting a divergence in policy in comparison with other disciplines, where analytical published papers are the overwhelmingly predominant form of output that is deemed to be acceptable as verifying international excellence. It is then down to the judgement of the expert panel members to decide the degree of international research content within these artefacts. This assessment normally has to be supported by evidence which may typically take the form of acceptance of an artwork for display in an internationally significant gallery, or commissioning of an artwork by a major client for an internationally recognised location. Similarly, creative works in the fields of the performing arts and broadcast media may also be accepted as being of international significance if they have been presented at an internationally recognised venue, event, or on an internationally respected media channel.

5.11 Monitoring and Audit

Audit is a major exercise in the UK every 4–5 years and is therefore a substantial incursion into the normal work of an institution. Consideration should be given to the cost/benefit of a more real-time evaluation of research utilising data that is already in the system (e.g. research grants awarded, PhD completions, papers published). A lighter touch, continuous monitoring, operating in the background should consume less resources, be more accurate at any point in time, and would make it more difficult for institutions to 'game-play', where considerable amounts of effort are put in to optimise a submission in order to obtain the best result possible – given that the funding results will last for the next 5 years.

5.12 Cost-Benefit Analysis

Finally, the opportunity-cost in the evaluation can be substantial. The question has been raised as to whether this is a wise use of resource that could otherwise have been spent in supporting new research. It has been estimated that academic and professional staff in institutions spent up to a year or more preparing their submissions. Panel members spent a year in analysing the submissions and preparing the results for publication. There are also the research opportunities lost by both of these parties essentially taking 2 years out of continuous research. Although the wide-ranging nature of the assessment provides testimony to its fairness and objectivity, if data is already in the system which could be used to give the same results to within 0.1 %, then questions can be asked about the overall cost-benefit balance of the process.

5.13 Changing Patterns of Publication

A further factor to consider is that the patterns of publication are changing and the implications of this need to be recognised. Many researchers are increasingly using the Internet and web not only to initiate collaborations with other researchers, but also to demonstrate and publish their work and generate impact. Many use blogs and Twitter to circulate ideas and generate interest. The term altmetrics was introduced to cover not just citation counts but also any form of reference or impact, such as how many data and knowledge bases refer to it, article views, downloads, references in blogs, social media, and news media [22]. Thus they can be applied not only to papers and books, but also to new kinds of output more appropriate to the web such as data sets, presentations, videos, source, repositories and web pages. With the increasing emphasis on open access and the increasing demand of sponsors and funding agencies to require researchers to provide the data underlying their research work, researchers are now often required to publish their data sets in conjunction with their paper.

Thus traditional printed and digital publications are being increasingly augmented by -

- *The sharing of "raw science" like datasets, code, and experimental designs.*
- *Semantic publishing or "nanopublication," where the citeable unit is an argument or passage rather than entire article.*
- *Widespread self-publishing via blogging, microblogging, and comments or annotations on existing work* [22].

5.14 Conclusions

The academic community in the UK recognises the importance of producing internationally leading outputs [23]. This in turn reflects the situation in most higher education institutions throughout the world. It is expected that research selectivity will continue to increase, and the future of research in most institutions other than those with the highest proportion of 4* and 3* research is unclear given that their QR funding is likely to decrease over time. It is clear that tactical decisions will continue to be made on whether to submit a selection of staff designed to maximise QR funding or reputation (highest possible scores) unless the rules change to make this impossible. However, it takes time and resource in order to make tactical decisions and tends to favour the larger institutions with more options to consider. This cost has to be added to the overall cost of the process.

Given that measures of impact may have been higher than expected overall, it is possible that in future more formal methods may be devised to evaluate impact more systematically on a rolling basis.

The increasing diversity of research outputs, and ways of evaluating them, provides an increasing opportunity for art and design to engage effectively in the ongoing discussions to ensure fair and equitable assessment of research quality in these areas, as well as their current and future resourcing.

The continued transition to the Internet and the availability of more real-time methods of evaluation may result in a changing landscape. Increasing selectivity in research and reductions in research funding imply that allocation of resource for research needs to be supported by evidence and cost-justified, and may no longer be allocated solely by periodic audit. It is possible therefore that real-time metrics may be used increasingly to monitor and review research progress and research quality, and also to provide navigation and management data for research development and delivery – on an individual, departmental, institutional, and national basis.

Further Reading

Andres, A.: Measuring Academic Research: How to Undertake a Bibliometric Study, p. 186. Chandos Publishing (2009)

Cronin, B., Sugimoto, C. R.:Beyond Bibliometrics: Harnessing Multidimensional Indicators of Scholarly Impact, p. 432. MIT Press (2014)

Pawson, R.: The Science of Evaluation: A Realist Manifesto. Sage (2013)

http://www.arc.gov.au/era/era_2010/archive/default.htm

http://www.arc.gov.au/era/era_2010/archive/key_docs10.htm

http://www.arc.gov.au/era/

References

1. How we fund research. HEFCE. http://www.hefce.ac.uk/whatwedo/rsrch/howfundr/
2. Evaluation of the research excellence framework – REF. http://www.hefce.ac.uk/whatwedo/rsrch/researchassessment/reffeedback/
3. Farla, K., Simmonds, P.: REF 2014 Accountability Review: Costs, Benefits and Burden. http://www.hefce.ac.uk/media/HEFCE,2014/Content/Pubs/Independentresearch/2015/REF, Accountability,Review,Costs,benefits,and,burden/2015_refreviewcosts.pdf
4. REF2014 Assessment Criteria and Level Definitions. http://www.ref.ac.uk/panels/assessmentcriteriaandleveldefinitions/ (2014)
5. Earnshaw, R.A.: Expanding the frontiers of visual analytics and visualization. In: Dill, J., Earnshaw, R.A., Kasik, D.J., Wong, P.C. (eds.) Knowledge Exchange, Technology Transfer and the Academy, pp. 469–480. Springer, London (2012). ISBN 978-1-4471-2803-9
6. Clark, B.: Creating Entrepreneurial Universities, International Association of Universities and Elsevier Science (1998)
7. Earnshaw, R. A., Liggett, S., Excell, P. S.: Evaluating the REF2014 results in art and design. Proceedings of Internet Technologies and Applications. For more information see: http://ita15.net/ita-art-expo/DownloadPDF (2015)
8. REF2014: Overview Report by Main panel D and Sub-panels 27–36, January 2015. http://www.ref.ac.uk/media/ref/content/expanel/member/Main%20Panel%20D%20overview%20report.pdf (2015)

9. REF2014: Submission data for Art and Design. http://results.ref.ac.uk/DownloadSubmissions/ByUoa/34
10. REF2014: Results for Art and Design: History, Practice and Theory. http://results.ref.ac.uk/Results/ByUoa/34
11. REF2014 – Results by Subject. http://www.timeshighereducation.co.uk/features/ref-2014-results-by-subject/2017594.article
12. REF2014: Average Profile for Art and Design. http://www.ref.ac.uk/media/ref/results/AverageProfile_34_Art_and_Design_History_Practice_and_Theory.pdf
13. Jump, P.: Cracking the Case Studies, pp. 32–41. Times Higher Education, 19 February 2015. http://www.timeshighereducation.co.uk/tablet/208D85EC/2018555.shared (2015)
14. Sayer, D.: Rank Hypocrisies: The Insult of the REF, p. 128, SAGE Publications Ltd. http://www.amazon.co.uk/Rank-Hypocrisies-Insult-SAGE-Swifts/dp/1473906563/ref=sr_1_3?s=books&ie=UTF8&qid=1425291891&sr=1-3&keywords=derek+sayer (2015)
15. Sayer, D.: One scholar's crusade against the REF. http://www.timeshighereducation.co.uk/features/one-scholars-crusade-against-the-ref/2017405.fullarticle
16. Mryglod, O., Kenna, R., Holovatch, Yu, Berche, B.: Predicting Results of the Research Excellence Framework Using departmental h-Index, Scientometrics, Springer, 23 December 2014. http://link.springer.com/article/10.1007/s11192-014-1512-3 (2014)
17. Welch, E.: Metrics in the Humanities: What Are We Measuring?, HEFCE Workshop, 16 Jan 2015. http://www.hefce.ac.uk/media/hefce/content/news/events/2015/hefcemetricsworkshopwarwick/Welch.pdf
18. Belfiore, E.: 'Impact', 'value' and 'bad economics': Making Sense of the Problem of Value in the Arts and Humanities. Arts and Humanities in Higher Education. ISSN 1474-0222. http://ahh.sagepub.com/content/14/1/95. http://ahh.sagepub.com/content/early/2014/04/22/1474022214531503.refs (2015)
19. REF2014, Panel Criteria and Working Methods. http://www.ref.ac.uk/media/ref/content/pub/panelcriteriaandworkingmethods/01_12_2D.pdf (2012)
20. White, H.D., Boell, S.K., Yu, H., Davis, M., Wilson, C.S., Cole, F.T.H.: Libcitations: a measure for comparative assessment of book publications in the humanities and social sciences. J. Am. Soc. Inf. Sci. Technol. **60**(6), 1083–1096 (2009). http://onlinelibrary.wiley.com/doi/10.1002/asi.21045/abstract
21. Independent review of the role of metrics in research assessment. http://www.hefce.ac.uk/rsrch/metrics/
22. Priem, J., Taraborelli, D., Groth, P. Neylon, C.: Altmetrics: a Manifesto, http://altmetrics.org/manifesto/ (2010)
23. Jump, P.: The Race Is Not to the Swift, pp. 35–59, Times Higher Education, 1 January 2015. http://www.timeshighereducation.co.uk/features/ref-2014-rerun-who-are-the-game-players/2017670.article (2015)

Printed in the United States
By Bookmasters